*Scio cui credidi*

*I know Whom I have believed*

2 Timothy Chapter 1 Verse 12

No matter what happens, I shall trust Him

1

# ONLY ONE THING WORSE

### HOW A FALSE ACCUSATION AFFECTED A LIFETIME

## by BETTE A. RICHARDS © 2020

**ONLY ONE THING WORSE**

To all those voices who are not heard


To my children, Ann, William, and Dala
who were my reason to go on


To my grandsons, Booker, Quinton, Malcolm, Joseph, William,
Nino, Michael, Tony, and granddaughter Jamie

# CONTENTS

# ACKNOWLEDGEMENTS

*Thanks to*

Dr. Don Beckstead

My brother, Dan Richards

My editor, Jim Krug

My dearest friend, Lee Thompson

My Life Coach, Joan McCall

My heartfelt appreciation to the others whose contributions

made this book's publication possible.

# E DI TOR'S  N OTE

Discrimination isn't white vs. black or black vs. white; prejudice is a spectrum, and we see Bette Richards run the gamut from one end to the other throughout her life.

I met Bette right before Christmas in 2015. This was a woman out of place, her nest sculpted from pieces of her life spanning New York City to Los Angeles, California.

I spent the last few years visiting her every month or so. Along the way, I learned of her passions and talent for music, and saw bits and pieces here and there of a book she was assembling about her life. Bette grew to trust me and I was honored to eventually edit her manuscript. You will be struck by the story itself.

But even more so, you will be struck by the depth and complexity of Bette's racial journey. After editing her manuscript, I feel what we are shown by the media today is overly simplified and polarizing. Race is not black and white, but many shades of grey, and you will see that in the pages that follow.

Her story will provide you a richer and more dynamic understanding of a true journey of race in America today.

Jim Krug, February 2019

## FOREWORD

This is a true story about a white girl in a small town in Pennsylvania along the Allegheny River. It reveals events describing an example of racial relations in America from a situation that is *rarely* discussed or examined.

The lack of exaggeration, propaganda and politics only adds to the authenticity of how one unfortunate event set the course in the lives of two innocent young victims.

It takes place in a small town in the mid-fifties where, up until then, there was a total lack of racial strife. I am witness to that fact, having some Negro playmates as a young boy in that town.

I never had a reason *not* to like someone of color. We lived near several very respectable families, some right across the street. As a young boy, the Powell family always purchased strawberries from me that I picked from my Grandparents' farm to sell to earn some money. They would also take me with them to the "Colored Elks Club" to see Ray Charles who was performing there with "The Clovers". I had a great time. My parents totally approved!

Mr. Johnston, our mailman, was the nicest, friendliest man whose two children were at the top of their class in my school. Maybe we were uninformed of the racial situation going on in the South. If at all, we must have felt far from it.

Then a rude awakening happened. The events revealed in this book became a shocking bit of reality. That was the 1950's! Then came the 60's and it all became political.


Dan Richards, Bette's brother

Santa Monica, CA

## INTRODUCTION

### *MY REASONS FOR WRITING THIS BOOK*

I am one of the voiceless.

I am a steel mill worker's daughter.

I did not and I do not have what Spike Lee calls in his film, JUNGLE FEVER.

I have never been put on anybody's pedestal nor do I want to be.

To my knowledge, no one has written about the *ostracization* of white women with mixed-race children.

A friend shared with me that when two of her black male friends read this manuscript and came to the part in the story where Cookie Gilchrist's chances to go to college were lost, they threw the pages down and would not read any further. They had no interest in what happens to the white woman.

It has been said to me "You made a *poor choice* in men".
I did not choose *them*.
I say, "The men chose me...for use at their pleasure".
And I, being "flattered" that I was chosen, complied with their wishes.

Nobody will write about this, so I have.

Bette Richards

# Chapter One

Pennsylvania 1954

**At a Police Station located in a town called New Kensington, Pennsylvania, situated along the Allegheny River eighteen miles north of Pittsburgh**

They were standing over me. First two of them, then three, then four, waving their fingers in my face.

"We're not going to have this in our town!"

"There's *only one thing worse* than a nigger, and that's a *nigger-lover.*"

"They're all crazy", I thought, as I stared at policemen whose faces were red with hate.

**Sunday School at First Church of God in Brackenridge, Pennsylvania**

The church woman called me "Little Jerry" because I look just like my Daddy, a spitting image of him. Several white children are in a circle, singing.

*Jesus loves the little children, All the children of the world*

*Red and yellow, black and white    They are precious in His sight*

*Jesus loves the little children of the world*

I am in the circle, five years old and singing my heart out.

"I can close my eyes and see Jesus. I want to marry him when I grow up", I said.

The Sunday School teacher tells us children about the ones who nailed Jesus to the cross and that we should learn to follow Jesus who said, "Father, forgive them for they know not what they do."

### Sheldon Park Projects in Natrona Heights, Pennsylvania, a small town twenty miles north of Pittsburgh

I'm playing with my dollhouse, I just got my period. No breasts yet. I could lose myself in that dollhouse. A world of make-believe. I moved the tiny furniture around with deep concentration. I had unlimited control.

Some other girls from the neighborhood were out on the lawn, twirling their batons and strutting back and forth. Everyone was practicing. There was going to be tryouts for the majorette corp. I went out to join them.

Later, I went to the tryouts just for the fun of it. There were about sixty girls there. All wearing shorts. I was the only one in blue jeans. My dad didn't allow *short* shorts. But I knew that I would never be chosen because all of the majorettes were older, and from the other side of town.

The following morning, my mother came into my bedroom and woke me.

"Someone just called and said that you're a 'majorette'. What's this all about? "

I could hardly believe it! They chose me!

"You know your dad won't let you…"

I pleaded with my mother to change Dad's mind. He did not want me showing bare legs in a majorette uniform.

I was frantic and begged, "Mom, *please* talk to Dad".

14

What caused him to change his mind and to allow me to go, I 'll never know. But, he finally said, "Okay".

Somehow my mother persuaded him.

~~~~~~~~~~~~~~~~

Har-Brack High Varsity Club, which was really "the football players," was throwing an initiation party for the new majorettes.

Dad did not want me going to any parties either.

Again, somehow my Mother persuaded him and he said that I could go. He drove me to the house party and would pick me up at 11pm. It was the first party in my life and I could hardly wait.

But, when I got there, I sat in a corner during the entire party, too shy to socialize. I watched the others when they slow-danced. The whole football team was there. Most of the girls were older than I.

Fullback Cookie Gilchrist was the star player, very popular and admired by everybody. He signed our Yearbooks with the same poem to everyone. He was scouted by just about every college and university in the country. He was a Negro. Everyone else there was white except for two other ball players.

During school, Cookie sat behind me in English class. He would tap on my shoulder, and I would move over a little to let him copy off of my test paper. Once he gave me tickets to one of the games, and I gave them to my Dad who loved football and took my little brother along to the game with him.

Cookie was leaving the party early and he asked, "Does anyone want a ride home?"

I was shy, sitting in a corner, and wanted to go home. So I piled into his car with several other kids.

He was dropping us off, one by one, until there were only two: another boy and me. Cookie asked if we were hungry. I nodded "Yes"; the other boy said "No." Cookie took him home.

I was last to be dropped off anyway, because I lived in Sheldon Park Projects, which was not far from where Cookie lived on Fourth Avenue along the railroad tracks. Most colored people lived there. It was known as "The Street".

Driving along, Cookie asked, "Your Dad work in the steel mill?"

I nodded, "Yes".

"Mine, too". There was no more talking between us. I was bashful and Cookie's mind seemed to be elsewhere and paying no attention to me.

But then he said, "I'm going where you can get a great hamburger; they put shredded cabbage on it". He turned on to the Tarentum Bridge crossing the Allegheny River heading into New Kensington, driving into a black section of town.

Cookie doubled-parked the car in front of McMillan's hamburger joint. He left me waiting in the car, telling me to keep the doors locked, and went inside.

A patrol car passed by. It stopped and shined a beam of light on me into the car. A policeman got out and came over to the window. He tapped on the window and I rolled it down. He asked to see my identification.

"I don't have any," I said.

"What are you doing in this neighborhood? Whose car is this?"

I was frightened and didn't answer.

Just then, Cookie came out carrying a small brown bag of hamburgers. He saw the police. He stopped in his tracks.

The policeman grabbed him, handcuffed him, threw him against the hood of the car spread-eagle and frisked him.

The other policeman got out of his car and removed me from Cookie's car. He handcuffed me, then put me in the back seat of the patrol car with Cookie.

They drove off to the police station as a crowd stood by and watched.

On the ride to the precinct, Cookie whispered to me, "Don't be afraid, Bette Ann, I'll get us out of this. Don't tell them your name. I know a lot of people and I'll get us out of this". He repeated, "I'll get us out of this".

Terrified now, I nodded, and thought, "Why do the police want him? What did he do?"

Inside the precinct, they sat me down way off in a corner. The police kept Cookie up front. They were questioning him, but it was too far away for me to make out what they were saying.

After a while, they took him through a door marked CELL ROOM. Then they brought me over to where they had questioned him. "What's your name?"

I was in shock, I did not answer. I thought, "Cookie said he would get us out of this…"

The police were standing over me, first two of them, then three, then four. They were angry and I was petrified.

"What are you doing with that nigger? There is only *one thing worse* than a nigger, and that's a *nigger-lover.* We are not going to have this in our town, nigger-lover," they snarled at me.

I thought, " What? What? Did Cookie do something?" They were waving their fingers in my face. They kept calling me "nigger-lover".

I said nothing, as I stared up at these men whose faces were red with hate. "You like that big, black dick, do you?"

Shocked and frightened, I froze. They said more. Sexual things. Things I never heard before and really didn't understand. They kept calling me "nigger-lover" over and over.

This went on and on, until I glanced up at a clock on the precinct wall. I saw that it was 2:30 in the morning. Dad said he would pick me up from the party at eleven, and I wasn't there.

Numbed with fear, I gave them my name, Bette Ann Richards.

A policeman asked, "What's your phone number?" I answered, "3177-J." He picked up the phone on the desk, slammed it down in front of me, and dialed.

"Hello, Mr. Richards. This is the New Kensington Police. "We caught your daughter parked with a nigger."

I didn't remember anything else until they took me through the same door Cookie had been taken through. They locked me in a cell. I curled up onto the steel slab.

Cookie was calling to me from his cell further down the way. He was calling loudly, "Don't be afraid. Don't worry, Bette Ann, I'll get us out of this." I did not respond.

18

I curled up into a fetal position on the iron green slab and closed my eyes.

I opened them to see through the jail bars, my Mom, my Dad, and a cop standing outside the cell.

My mother wailed, "This sight will be before me for the rest of my life… my daughter behind bars."

The policeman said, "We have the nigger down here." They all three walked away from my cell toward Cookie's cell.

"Don't you know you're a nigger?" Dad was yelling at Cookie. "What are you doing with my daughter?"

Cookie defiantly said, "I'll go with *your* daughter," then pointing to the policeman, "*his* daughter, or *anyone's* daughter that I please".

I heard them argue back and forth, but my senses were shutting down, then I didn't hear another word.

The next thing I recalled was standing in front of a policeman's desk with my parents. The policeman was saying that I would have to return for a hearing the next morning. They wanted to examine me to "see if I had sex." They said I would be sent to a reform school. They said "*because we're not having this in our town.*"

When we left, going down the Precinct steps, my mother came between me and my dad, stopping him as he tried to knock me down.

Timid and introverted from childhood, I stayed silent. I thought of what I had heard in my Sunday School class about Jesus… "He opened not His mouth".

I don't remember anything more after that.

I was later told that my Mother saw to it that a sexual examination did not take place.

The next time I went to school, somebody wrote in lipstick on the mirror in the girl's bathroom, "Bette Ann was out with Cookie Gilchrist last night…".
It spread all over town that Cookie and I were "caught together and went to jail."
One rumor even said that we were caught parked "naked."

Threatening phone calls began coming to my home. "We're gonna get you, nigger-lover. We're gonna tar and feather you."

When I walked to school, the boys would throw stones at me. They would spit at me and yell, "Hey, nigger-lover!"

I closed my eyes…taking it in silence like Jesus did… "Father, forgive them, for they know not what they do, Father, forgive them. Please."

Cookie wasn't in school anymore. His father got him out of town because of the threats to lynch him.

He accepted an offer from the Cleveland Browns and won "Rookie of the Year" in the NFL in 1954. So, Cookie never got to go to any of the colleges or universities and accept their offers.

I did not see him again until several years later.

`\\\\\\\`

The school principal called me into his office. He asked if Cookie was my boyfriend. I moved my head slowly, "No". I told him that the majorettes wanted to throw me out the corps. This made him angry.

He took me out to the football field where they were having majorette practice drills. He told them, "She has not done anything wrong. The boy is just 'different'. If you majorettes won't have her, then the whole corps is disbanded!" Nobody said a word. Through all of this, he was the only one who ever stood up for me.

So, I went to the majorette practices and marched in all the football games at half time. I went to all my classes and made good grades. I rode on the majorette bus to all the "away" games, but no one sat next to me. There was always an empty seat beside me. No one spoke to me and I did not speak a word to anyone for many months. A Sunday School song would run constantly in my head…"If your heart keeps right… if your heart keeps right…" I still did not open my mouth. I had learned in Sunday School that all things come from God's hands, so I was silent and accepted it.

# Chapter Two

HOLY MOSES, I HAVE BEEN REMOVED

(from *Border Song* by Elton John/Bernie Taupin)

## Aftermath

Dad is razzed and taunted at the steel mill by the other workers.

"Your daughter is a nigger-lover."

Dad comes home from work, covered with dirt from the steel mill. I am sitting alone at the kitchen table, doing my homework. He slams his lunch bucket down on the table. He comes over to me and grabs a handful of my hair, pulling my head back. He calls my mother, my brother, my sister…" Get in here!! She ruined the Richards' good name."

My mother is putting wet clothes through the wringer of the wash tub in the Utility Room right next to the kitchen. My brother and sister come running down the stairs and stop at the banister. My Dad, still with my hair in his fist, pulls my head back and says to them, "Hit her in the face till she says 'nigger'. Make her say 'nigger'. Come on! It's your name, too!"

My brother and sister are peeking through the banister, huddled together, motionless. Mother punches me in my back while my Dad held my head. I cringe.

But I kept silent and would not open my mouth.

At Kipp's, a small convenience store in Tarentum, my little sister is playing on the steps. She sprains her ankle. When she goes into that store for help, they think she is me and they spit on her.

Mother is combing my sister's hair. "How pretty you are!" she tells my sister. Mother turns toward me…"You. It will be hard for anyone to love *you*." I disappear to hide in a remote part of the house.

My mother comes into my bedroom to wake me for school. She shakes me. "Get up, nigger-lover, shame on you! You have ruined the Richards name."

From then on, my parents ignored me as if I did not exist. Around and around in my head I heard , "When my father and mother forsake me, the Lord will take me up." (Psalms 27:10)

Years later, I wondered what pain this all caused my father who had loved me. When I pleaded my case to go to the party, he gave in to my mother, allowing me to have my desire.

~~~~~

After high school, I worked at a movie theater in the ticket booth, as a salesgirl at a department store, and on an assembly line where I cleaned parts for home appliances.

However, I still kept to myself. White kids would have nothing to do with me. Some time after high school graduation, one of the best-looking white boys in town called me one afternoon and asked me if I would like to go for a ride! I was surprised and puzzled, because nobody ever asked me to go anywhere or to do anything with them thinking the way they did that I was "bad because I was a "nigger-lover".

I accepted his invitation. He picked me up at my house and drove me to Cookie who was in town visiting his folks. Cookie had been in Canada and playing football for the Hamilton Tiger Cats.

This guy was "going" with Cookie's cousin and Cookie had asked him to pick me up and bring me to him.

Cookie talked to me as one who was concerned. "You know, there is no life for you in this town, Bette Ann. You should leave here."

His compassion moved me and my heart ached, but I would just stare at him and still had no words to respond.

From then on, when Cookie would come back from Canada, he would call me to ask how I was doing. Some afternoons, I would walk down the road to meet him.

One time, he came in a shiny black Thunderbird with the tire on the trunk. He insisted I try it out and he showed me how to drive it. (My Dad had already taught me how to drive his Chevy.)

Sometimes Cookie would take me with him to music clubs in the Hill District of Pittsburgh for matinees. This is when I first heard live black musicians and I felt a kinship with them.

Cookie was the only one with whom I had any connection…the only one who showed any concern for me. I was still extremely shy and hardly spoke at all.


At home, in bed at night I listened to music on my brown plastic record player. I kept it right at the head of my bed.

And I read a lot: Philosophy books and the Bible (only Proverbs), but rarely ever fiction.

One day I was in the music store choosing records. Count Basie, Nat King Cole, the Clovers, Moonglows, James Brown and the Flames. They were called sepia records. On the bus back home, some teenagers knew who I was and demanded to see what I had in my bag. They grabbed it, looked at those records and started to taunt me….nigger music, nigger lover….and broke every one of them into pieces.

~~~~~~~~~~~~~~~~~~

Cookie made another return visit to Pennsylvania. He called, and I walked out of the house to meet him. He would talk to me like a protective, big brother. He drove us to a jazz club, The Crawford Grill in the Hill District of Pittsburgh.

When I returned home, I went into my bedroom that I shared with my sister. As I walked through the room, I brushed past her. She started to fuss. When dad heard our raised voices, he came charging in. "What's going on in here, you nigger-lover? You were with that nigger! I know who you were with!  I had you followed."

Something finally snapped in me. I stared into my father's eyes.  Then I said slowly… "He's *NOT A NIGGER* and so I am *NOT* a *NIGGER-LOVER*."

Why did I dare talk back to him? You did not talk back to my father. He smashed me in the mouth with his fist, knocking my teeth loose. I had never harmed a living thing in my life, and where this came from, only God knows, but I made a small fist and hit him back in his chest.

He went berserk and punched me over and over again, until I fell down across my bed. He took off his belt and began beating me. He was in a rage, but I would not show any emotion. Mom burst into the room, screaming, "Stop! You're killing her!" You're going to kill her!"

My mother pulled him off me and they left the room. Blood welts and bruises were all over my body. I picked myself up, put on my raincoat, and walked down the road to find a phone booth to call Cookie at his cousin's home. He was leaving to go back to Canada. He had been telling me over and over, "you have no life in this town, Bette Ann."

I told him what happened and said, "I'll leave, now, Cookie."

He said, "Go to the Western Union and wait," He would wire some money.

I was emotionally numb.

I took a cab twenty-two miles to the Pittsburgh airport and flew to Canada.

*On the airplane, my mind went way back to my daddy sitting in his easy chair, reading the newspaper. At five years old, I bring one of my dolls to him. I'm wearing the heart-shaped pendant he made for me out of scraps from the steel mill. He puts down his paper and smiles. I lay the dolls one by one in his arms. I bring him another. Then, another and another until he has all my dolls spread across both his open arms. He's watching his little girl with eyes full of love.*

Still covered in bruises, I took a taxi from the airport to Cookie's address. I gazed at a gorgeous Canadian sunset as I sped along the Queens Highway towards Hamilton, Ontario.

At Cookie's house, he partied most of the time with his two teammates and with various women visitors. I sat in corners most of the time and just watched, detached and alone. The women were beautiful and sexy. Although I was probably the same age, I viewed them as "grown-up". I still felt like a child and had no desire to join in. I was deep in a shell by now, and only music could draw any emotion.

Cookie learned that my name was on the Missing Persons List. There was no trace of me.

After two weeks in Canada, Cookie urged me to call my home to let them know my whereabouts. This terrified me. He reassured me that they could not do anything to me, get to me, or hurt me.

He brought me the phone. I dialed with Cookie at my side. My mother answered and became hysterical. I hung up.

Cookie insisted that I call right back; I did not want to, but he insisted.

Mother answered again. "I have been worried sick", she said, "I thought I'd lost my daughter; we thought you jumped off the Tarentum Bridge. I'll try to understand if you love him."

"...*Mother thinks I love him*", I thought. I felt nothing; I listened but gave no response.

She asked me to come home.

"What about Dad?"I said.

"I'll talk to Dad. Just come home."

I wanted to go home.

Cookie bought the ticket.

I flew home to Pennsylvania, and returned to my father's house,

 I had no where else to go.

Days and months passed.

Dad ignored me as if I weren't there, as if I didn't exist.

Alone in a complete sense, I stayed in my room or in remote parts of the house away from my father.  Whichever room he was in, I made sure I was in another room. I made myself invisible, stayed out of sight, and began to master the art of disappearing.

~~~~~~~~~~~~~~~~~~

Sometime much later, Cookie came to Pennsylvania to visit his folks again and was trying to reach me all day.  I had gone to a matinee at a jazz club in Pittsburgh with an older woman friend.

When I got home late that evening, the phone rang. It was Cookie.  He was upset. I had always been there before when he called.

 He wanted to know where I had been. He had become protective and sounded possessive like my father.

I wouldn't tell him.

He said he was coming right out there.  When Cookie's car came flying up the dirt road to my house, I went out to meet him because I was afraid it would wake my father.

"Get in!" he demanded. He drove out to the country on a backwoods road and stopped the car by a field. It was pitch dark. He reached across me to the glove compartment, and took out a gun. He loaded it, slowly.

"Where were you and who were you with, Bette Ann?" I sat there motionless, staring straight ahead.

He played with the gun as he asked again and again, "Who were you with?" At first I said nothing. I thought, *"What is wrong with him? Why is he acting like this?"* Then I started to make something up.

"You're lying, Bette Ann…" He pulled the trigger back, then turned and shot it out the car window into the field.  Neither of us said a word.

He started the car, and took off, driving recklessly around the winding dirt road. I was terrified. What was he going to do?

We went flying around a sharp curve and the car went out of control.  I was leaning against the passenger door.  The right rear fender slammed against the side of a tree trunk. The door flew open and I flew out, head first. The car kept going, then finally stopped.

Cookie got out. He walked back to where I was lying and picked me up in his arms. I had cuts on my head all through my scalp.

He could not take me to a hospital, so he took me to his relatives who quietly cleaned me up. He told them, "All I could see were her shoes going out the door".

 I was silent through it all.  And neither of us spoke a word to each other as Cookie drove me back home.

I couldn't move my neck for a long time. I still never opened my mouth. I let my mother believe a cold had left me with a stiff neck.

I closed down even more.

*Put your hands in His, BetteAnn, and hold on, hold on, I kept praying.*

**Practicing for the try-outs**

Chester "Cookie" Gilchirst is our player of the year. He has been named to the Fullback position an all W. P. I. A. L. AA all-star teams. "Cookie" is all-state A.P., U.P., Sun-Tele player of the year, the highest scoring Back in Western Pennsylvania with 186 points, and the recipient of the Stanwix Award, a local honor.

As a full-fledged Har-Brack High School majorette.

***Cookie Gilchrist***
**Har-Brack High School football hero**

**Gilchrist and his Dad show the
feelings of the community.**

# Gilchrist Signs with Browns

The professional Cleveland Browns of the National Football League today announced signing Chester Gilchrist, a high school junior who won't be 19 until next month.

Gilchrist, a 200-pound fullback, led Har-Brack High School through an unbeaten season in 1953 and was named to the All-Pennsylvania scholastic team.

Commissioner Bert Bell of the National Football League gave the Browns special permission to sign the boy, who will be ineligible to play for Har-Brack High School next season.

Bell acted upon advice from Gilchrist's high school principal, Walter S. Bazard, who said the boy "has no college aspirations or intentions." The school principal said it would be "a real break" for the boy to have a chance at pro football.

Gilchrist will report to the Browns' training camp next month. Coach Paul Brown said it would be "an unusual case if Gilchrist makes our team, but the boy has great speed, is big and strong and appears to be the type of boy who reaches a peak early in his football career."

No mention was made of the duties Gilchrist will take over with the Browns or the salary. Previous stories had him signing for approximately $5,500 a year.

Gilchrist's defensive ability and place-kicking will undoubtedly be given top consideration by the Cleveland club. Although it has been through his offensive action that he has become best known, Gilchrist held the Har-Brack squad together defensively through its recent unbeaten season. His line-backing was the envy of every coach in the Class AA ranks.

Over 40 of his 186 points last season were extra-point placement kicks.

# Chapter Three

## JERRY'S DAUGHTER

## Childhood in Pennsylvania

My father, Gerald "Jerry" Ira Richards, came from a line of hard-working men. His family originally was from Wales, Ireland, and England.

With only an eighth-grade education, he landed in the CCC (Civilian Conservation Corps), a Depression-era employment program.  He was later hired at Allegheny Ludlum Steel Mill in Brackenridge, Pennsylvania,  a small town on the Allegheny River twenty miles north of Pittsburgh.  His position was a grimy job in the white-labor paint gang.  It was separated from the black-labor gang of Negro men. He climbed smoke stacks and did all the dirty work in the cinder pits, and after coming home every day covered with black soot, he would have two bottles of his Pabst Blue Ribbon beer.

Jerry was a steel mill worker for 38 years who voted Republican every election. Forced to join the Union, he angrily resented the dues taken out of his paycheck.

My mother, Ann Betush, the oldest of ten siblings, was raised on the farm that her father, John Betush, purchased after he entered the United States through Ellis Island. The eighty-five acre farm was in Tarentum, a town located next to Brackenridge.
 He was born in Czechoslovakia and had married my grandmother, who was born in Budapest, Hungary, and also came to America through Ellis Island.

Pappap, as we called him, also worked in the coal mines. Some of the men in the family were hunters and fishermen, and my mother served many a meal of rabbit and deer meat. But a favorite of mine was Mom's Hungarian paprika chicken with home-made noodles. Like my father, my mother, too, had only an eighth grade education.

One year and twelve days after my mother married my father, she went into labor in the middle of the night. There were no telephones. No doctor could be reached, so a veterinarian horse doctor was summoned to the tiny bedroom of the house on Ninth Avenue, Brackenridge.

I was born on a Good Friday before Easter Sunday. Dad wanted to name me Beatrice. Mom objected because that was the name of his old girlfriend. They settled for the name "Bette Ann".

Three years later, we moved to a house on Bull Creek Road in the outskirts of the nearby town, Tarentum, where my brother, Danny, was born  A year after that, we moved to a section of town called Creighton Hollow and into my Czech great-grandmother's house. That was where my sister, Esther, was born.

I was still the apple of my Daddy's eye.

Later the family moved to a two-bedroom apartment in Sheldon Park, a government project in Natrona Heights just over the hill. We three siblings slept in one tiny bedroom, a room so small that it held only bunk beds and a cot on which I slept in the middle of the room.

Soon after, we transferred to a three-bedroom and now my sister and I shared a room. It was a four-family building with a front and back yard. Eventually, my mom wanted to buy a house to get us out of the projects. When she asked a rich aunt for a loan, her aunt refused and said, "Your husband is not good for anything. He is not handy. All he can do is *sing*."

Dad had an absolutely beautiful tenor voice and some women at church were always fawning over him because of his powerful singing.

My mom left her father's Baptist church for my dad's Church of God. When she attended for the first time, she noticed Dad in the choir as he sang a solo. He noticed her beautiful thick, brown hair, and the attraction was immediate.

Our family rarely missed a Sunday service, Bible study every Wednesday and Prayer meeting on Friday. When Dad had to work some Sundays, Mom took us to church on the bus.

At the age of 10, I proudly ironed Dad's white shirts for church and packed his lunch for work every day.

At dinner, we had to be quiet…no talking at the table. It was an era when children were seen but not heard. But, nevertheless, when mom and dad would argue I would say: "Daddy, don't talk to Mommy like that," and, "Mommy, don't talk to Daddy like that".

I would watch my mother clip coupons from the newspaper… save five cents, ten cents, and so forth, and I swore I would never waste precious time in my life by cutting out coupons. But counter to what I felt as a child, today I realize that I myself do sometimes engage in this ignoble task.

There was no health insurance and Mom gave us children Paregoric for just about any and every ailment.

Dad wanted me to learn to play the piano and he paid for lessons for me. Mom was not happy with the expense and she, at first, objected. The lessons would cost three dollars an hour, but she finally agreed to a half lesson a week for a dollar-fifty because Dad insisted. Then he bought a spinet piano on time. Yet when I wanted a big baby doll for Christmas, which was very expensive, Mom bought it for me but told me I needed to hide the doll from Daddy. To keep it a secret, I kept it hidden under my bed and could only play with it when my daddy wasn't at home.

I studied piano from fourth grade to seventh grade, and then I could accompany dad when he sang his solos. Each Christmas, I played the piano as he sang "O Holy Night" at church. He often brought new sheet music home for me to learn, especially, Irish songs like "Too Rah Loo Rah Loo Rah." I'd play and he'd sing.

Dad would take us children to tent revivals and camp meetings where we learned many gospel songs. Mom's four brothers had a gospel singing group with one of my uncles playing lead guitar.

~~~~~~~~~~~~~~~~~~

Playing out in the yard one day, I found a rosary in the grass. I thought it was a necklace. I hung it around my neck. When I went into the house, my mother saw it. She said, "Where did you get that? Take that off! "

"But, I found Jesus, Mommy! it's Jesus, Jesus on the cross, Mommy!"

Mom said angrily, "He is not on the cross anymore! Take it off!." Then she took it away from me.

One day, while reading a verse from the Bible, the word "faith" stood out from the page, and I saw a circle of bright light flashing around it. It seemed like it was shining with an inner light.

34

Every Sunday after church, my mom cooked a full-course dinner. And after the meal, we drove off to Pappap Betush's farm in Tarentum. At the age of five, I would get out of the car and run to a large patch of violets circling a big tree. It was my favorite spot where I would carefully pick a bouquet of violets, run over and proudly present them to my daddy.

When I was in the fifth grade, my English teacher told the class, "Bette Ann wrote the best opening sentence ever and what did Bette Ann do? She drew a line through it, crossed it out, then wrote a very ordinary one instead." I was extremely shy and did not want attention drawn to me. I was petrified to talk in front of others and did not want to stand out.

When I was twelve years old, our whole family went on a rare vacation to Birmingham, Alabama, to visit Dad's brother, Uncle Lyle. We took the trip in Dad's 1936 stainless steel Ford. He didn't know that car would be worth a million dollars to collectors one day, and Dad was swindled into selling it to a salesman from the Allegheny Ludlum Steel Company where Dad was working. Dad asked for a trade for a new Chevrolet, but ended up accepting just one hundred dollars.

My brother, Danny, loved that car and had dreamed of driving it when he was older.

Arriving in Birmingham, we stopped at a park to have a picnic; I walked over toward a water fountain. My parents told me, "You cannot drink from that fountain because the sign says COLORED". I thought it meant that the water would come out in colors.

When I was 13, Dad brought home from work a beautiful acrylic heart on a chain, filled with shimmering metal shavings ground from steel. He made it at the mill. Mom thought it was for her.

But he gave it to me.

Sometimes Dad went golfing at a public course on weekends. He took me with him a few times and gave me some golf lessons.

Education was not a priority with my parents, so they wanted me to quit school when I reached 16, the legal age to go to work at a factory, to bring in some money. My grades were As and Bs on the Honor Roll but it did not matter to them. My teachers objected to my quitting, so I stayed in school.

I was always singing around the house. And anything I sang…. there would be my little sister, Esther, harmonizing with me. Our music together seemed to have a life of its own. My sister had a gift for harmony like no other. Washing and drying the dishes…we would be singing. Lying in our beds at night, we would be singing. We loved sitting on the bank of Bull Creek kicking our feet in the water…. singing away.

My little brother, Danny, was a typical boy who got into mischief. These were the days when parents could whip their children, and if you did't kill them, nothing happened to you.

I had to watch Danny get lots of 'lickins' from dad. Sometimes he would get beaten outside in front of the neighbors and I would cry for my little brother. I, myself, was not afraid of my dad because I never got into trouble with him, as I was a very obedient daughter.

Mom never once interfered or tried to stop Dad from beating Danny. However, she always took up for Esther. Mom dressed Esther in pretty dresses and put flowers in her hair. Esther got anything she wanted from Mom, and I had to let my little sister have anything of mine that she desired. Mom would say to me, "Give it to your baby sister, Bette Ann, you are a good girl." I really did not mind much because I always wanted to please my mom. Then she would often recite this poem by Henry Wadsworth Longefellow from a Little Golden Book of poetry:

> "There was a little girl
>
> *Who had a little curl*
>
> *Right in the middle of her forehead*
>
> *And when she was good*
>
> *She was very, very good*
>
> *And when she was bad*
>
> *She was horrid"*

Dad was a strict disciplinarian. When he told us kids to do something and we asked "Why?", he would yell "Because I said so!" And that was that!

When we kids were joking around with one another and having fun, Dad would order us to calm down and shut up the noise. We had to curb our enthusiasm. I learned well how to do that.

Years later, when my dad died, I thought about his hard life of 38 years in that steel mill, and how his fellow workers made fun of him and belittled him because he had no education. I would cry for my father.

But, how he loved to sing!

# Chapter Four

RESURRECTION

O! Booker

Pittsburgh &  New York      Baby Girl Ann


Cookie introduced me to musicians at the clubs. I was 19 years old now and I began traveling by myself on the bus from New Kensington to Pittsburgh.

One afternoon I was invited by drummer J. C. Moses. whom I had met at one of the matinees with Cookie, to J. C.'s mother's house in the Hill District for an afternoon rehearsal. I was deeply tanned and wore a white cotton dress with a halter top. When J.C. introduced me, he said, "She looks like Ava Gardner!".

His drums were set up in the living room. It was large and sparsely furnished, with unfinished dark wooden floors. There were other musicians there and they were "jammin". When J.C. hinted about sex, I told him that I never did that before. He was astounded, and then treated me like a sister. Later, when he introduced me to anyone, he said "this is my heart", and he was from then on, protective of me.

I met Chuck Jackson there, who was rehearsing with the band. He was called Charles then and fame had not yet found him. Later, he recorded the song, *Any Day Now,* and it was a big hit. Chuck introduced me to black artists such as Jackie Wilson, Sam Cook, and the doo-wop group called the Platters when they were performing in Pittsburgh.

~~~~~~~~~~~~~~~~

Some months later, I went to hear a fantastic drummer, Max Roach and his group at the Crawford Grill, a famous meeting place for musicians in the Hill District of Pittsburgh. They were in town from New York for a two-week engagement.

As I walked into the club, my eyes were drawn to one of the musicians up on the bandstand.

He was holding his trumpet in his hand.

Our eyes met.

He came down from the stage and walked straight over toward me.

He introduced himself.

His name was Booker Little.

I found him indescribably beautiful.

I stayed with him in his room at the Ellis Hotel for the entire two-week engagement. He took me to his bed, laid me down, and like an obedient child, I did not protest. He held me gently like you hold a child. And I let him have his way with me.

He was shocked to learn that he had taken my virginity.

During our love-making, I felt all of his power, intensity, his gentleness and it made me want to call out the name of Sweet Jesus!

At that moment Booker became locked in my heart and my mind.

Through Booker's eyes, I felt loved. He knew nothing of my past. But he sensed that I could not see myself at all. On one occasion, he stopped to gaze at the two of us in the hallway mirror as we walked into his room. He took me over to the dresser mirror to show me what he saw, and told me I was beautiful. My face, my legs. He loved the way I dressed... simple, classic. He assumed that I was from a wealthy family, and I did not say a word. He complimented my long-sleeved white silk blouse, gray wool skirt. And high, high heels.

When he pulled me over to him and took me into his arms, it was divine….Heaven.

Booker was my mirror. He reflected his vision of me and I was radiant in his presence. Booker's beauty began a redeeming of the horror of my past, like the awakening of a dead child.

~~~~~~~~~

Our birthdays were only one week apart.

One night in the hotel room he played "Moonlight Becomes You" on his trumpet especially for me.

Another time, I cut my hand and wanted to ignore it. "It's nothing," I said.

"No, no! That's the only hand you will ever have," he said as he gently took my hand and held it softly against his face.

~~~~~~~~~

Booker's nickname was "BEE TEE" (Booker Taliaferro Little, Jr.), named after Booker T. Washington.

From a well-to-do musical family in Memphis, his father played trombone in the Baptist Church and his sister sang in the London Opera Company. Booker studied at the Conservatory of Music in Chicago at the age of fifteen. He became a virtuoso on the trumpet.

Booker lived and breathed music and was arranging and composing most of the time. "There are no wrong notes," he would often say.

I loved it when he talked to me about freedom, needing freedom to say all that we want to say, and about how much work there was in perfecting ourselves. We discussed other musicians and the self-destruction of some. He told me that he was more conservative than many of his friends. About Duke Ellington, orchestra leader, pianist and composer, he said, "He is the last word." Booker told me about the "true people and the not so true".

One time, we went to the Musicians Club in Pittsburgh. I was pleased to see a dance floor there. "I do not dance. I never took the time to learn", Booker explained. He neither drank nor smoked.

Once, at another all-black club in Pittsburgh, as we were getting seated, Max Roach and Abbie Lincoln came by. Abbie had been a cabaret singer but was now a jazz singer who wore her hair in an Afro-natural style. Booker spoke to her and he turned and started to introduce me. She turned her nose up and walked away as I tried to speak to her. It was the first encounter with black women where I would be shunned.

But it wasn't by far the last. I saw the pain black women endure when they see a white woman whom they believe is "taking their man".

~~~~~~~~~~~~~~~~~~

The gig at the Crawford Grill was over now. Booker left Pennsylvania and went back to New York.

Four months passed.

My mother noticed my growing belly and sat me down at the kitchen table. "Are you pregnant?" she asked.

"I haven't had my period in four months", I replied.

42

Mom stared at me and said, " You will have to have an abortion".

I shook my head…" No!" I yelled. Because we were Christians, I was shocked that my mother said such a thing.

Mom said, "Then you have to *get out of this house*; Dad will kill you."

She assumed it was Cookie's baby. I said nothing.

~~~~~~~~~~~~~~~~~~~

Time passed. I kept to myself in my room. My brother told me years later that I had stayed for a short period with a colored family in Arnold, PA, a nearby town. I don't remember how I got there. It is most likely that my mother had arranged it.

My mother worked for Bernice Miller who was selling her beauty salon and moving to New York City. I knew the woman because my sister and I sometimes would help our mother clean the salon. Unbeknownst to me, arrangements were made between my mother and Bernice to take me with her to New York.

~~~~~~~~~~~~~~~~~~~

I found myself in New York at Bernice's apartment on 84th Street and West End Avenue with no memory of how I got there. Conscious memory requires language and I had no words for what I was going through.

Bernice was gone during the day, working at her job, and she went out to clubs and parties at night.

I spent night after night alone in the apartment.

I was in a deep sleep…detached, oblivious, withdrawn.

At eight months, my water broke. I went to the Emergency Room at Metropolitan Hospital and my complications began. When three days passed without labor starting,

The doctors said that I could not return home because an infection had set in that could affect the baby. I had to stay on bed-rest.

Almost a month later they tried to induce labor two different times. Contractions occurred for hours and hours, but nothing happened. The doctors decided to forcibly pull the baby out. I hemorrhaged and ended up in a coma for three days.

When I came to, an orderly shaking his head, told me, "Boy oh boy, you had a close call".

It was the 21st of November when Ann Carla Bett was born. She was already three days old when I first held her, because I was unconscious for three days after giving birth.

I gave her the name, Ann, after my Czech great-grandmother whom I loved so much, Carla, after my favorite uncle Carl Betush, and Bett, as part of myself.

I have a vague memory of my mother and sister standing at the foot of my hospital bed. They had come to visit.

Booker knew nothing of any of this and I didn't even tell him I was now in New York.

I was ashamed.

I left the hospital after thirty-one days with my new, beautiful baby girl. I have no recollection of coming back from the hospital to the apartment on 84th Street and West End Avenue. But I do remember when going home from the hospital, my baby Ann's cradle was an empty dresser drawer.

I would go on outings with Ann to Riverside Park, spread blankets on the grass, and spend many lonely days with her there.

When taking Ann to the baby clinic for her check-up, I watched a woman sitting across from me. She seemed serene and secure and sure of herself. I sat transfixed as I compared myself to her calmly and slowly unwrapping her baby to tend to it. And I felt unsure, inadequate, and very lonely.

Getting off the subway, as I walked on 84th Street to the apartment, Louie McKay, Billie Holliday's husband, passed us carrying Billie's white chihuahua. Billie had passed away about six months earlier at the hospital where Baby Ann was born. He noticed my brown baby, stopped, and said how beautiful the baby was. He took my baby's hand and placed a folded five dollar bill into it.

~~~~~~~~~~~~~~~~~~~

I was now living at the Lanseer Hotel on 51st Street around the corner from Birdland.

Mom and Dad came to New York to see my sister who was always my mother's favorite. Dad learned that I had a baby and wanted to see me. When they came, Dad saw Baby Ann, now three months old, lying on the bed.

"That baby is *black*!" he yelled. He called to Mom, "Come out of here!" They left without another word.

Back in Pennsylvania, Dad caught Mom putting some money in an envelope to send to me. He took the money out, then tore up the letter.

~~~~~~~~~~~~~~~~~~~

One day as I was out walking carrying my baby, a musician friend, Sonny Redd, passed by. He said, "Beautiful baby! Who's the daddy?"

"Booker Little", I answered.

"I bet Booker is proud of her! Booker spit her out!"

I paused. "Booker doesn't know about her ."

"What?! You're not right! Booker is not that kind of man. He should know that he has a child. Will you let me tell him about her?" he asked.

"Yes." I replied.

The next day there is a knock at my door.

I open it.

Booker is standing there.

My heart opens wide.

Booker pulls me to him and he cradles me in his arms.

When he sees his baby girl, he opens her pink blanket slowly and lovingly examines and touches every inch of her whole little body, gently squeezing her tiny arms and legs.

"I'm glad she is in this world," he says.

Baby Ann looks just like her daddy!

He kisses us both.

~~~~~~~~~~~~~~~~~

Booker gave me the photo of himself taken at the photography studio for the cover of his album, "Victory and Sorrow". It was the shot he said they would not use... he was wearing sunglasses.

That photo is the only item I have now that his hands have touched.

He sometimes had a Monday night gig at Birdland which paid $20. He would give me $5. He said that the money was for Baby Ann's formula.

Booker came often to see us. As he was playing with his baby one day, he commented, "This is a *big tie... a big tie*".

My heart dropped. I knew what that meant.

Full of shame, I would not "restrain" him for a moment. I would not burden him.

Afraid to reveal myself, and because I knew that he assumed I came from a family of money and class, I took our baby and ran away...I moved out and left no forwarding address.

When he visited again, we were gone. Later, when I went back to the hotel for my mail, he had left a note in the mailbox asking for us.

I moved into an apartment in Brooklyn with my brother and sister, and never saw Booker again.

The great pianist, Wynton Kelly, a neighbor, lived next door. As he was sitting on the stoop next to my apartment building, he watched Ann playing outside.
He shook his head and commented, "Booker spit her out!"

~~~~~~~~~~~~~~~~~~~

While still living in Brooklyn, I received a phone call..."Booker died".

I have no recollection of who it was who called. And I didn't believe this.
I said, "This is *not funny...*".

I remember nothing after that, except when Booker's friend, saxophonist George Coleman, visited. I had condemned myself for my loss and he tried to comfort me by telling me, "Booker thought the world of you."

Booker was the mirror to my soul. In my heart, everything next to God Himself. With him gone, any bit of hope in me felt lost.

47

After he died, I just survived.

The media called the cause of death uremia, but I think it was George who told me it was lupus erythematous, an auto immune disease that just eats you away. Booker was just 23.

~~~~~~~~~~~~~~~~~~

There was a memorial for Booker at the Five Spot Cafe in New York. I wandered through the crowded club anonymously. Many famous people were there. Duke Ellington was standing in the middle of the packed room. As I passed by him, our eyes met, locked, and held for a few moments as if he saw into the depths of my soul. Then someone came up and spoke to him, calling his attention away. I continued walking on through the crowd as if I were invisible.

Back home in my room, my thoughts were whirling.

Booker was the only one who ever really saw me.

Nevermore. Never again. Nothing left.

*I saw his smile. Remembered his voice saying to me…"Sleep well".*

Finally, and the only time through it all, I cried. The tears started to pour out of my eyes. Gut-wrenching sobs. Then, that piercing howl of pain.

~~~~~~~~~~~~~~~~~~

Over the next few years, my brother went back to Pennsylvania and I moved with my sister and Baby Ann to a one-room apartment on 10th Avenue in Hell's Kitchen. I found jobs in offices and worked as a file clerk at first. Promotions to billing clerk and secretary soon followed.

I carried Baby Ann on the subway, getting off, walking her to the Puerto Rican babysitter, then back to the subway, crowded like sardines, where I couldn't move because of people crushed up against me. I only worked in those offices to exist and to take care of my child.

Where did all this leave me? With no identity of my own.

Exiled now. *By* my *own choice.* Feared and repulsed by whites, excluded and discounted, and mostly ignored by blacks. My feelings dead.

My instincts were to align with the oppression of black lives.

But I wasn't black.

Yet the experience of ostracism and oppression which I endured for being in the company of the black male, of being a white woman, of raising black babies, was very similar.

~~~~~~~~~~~~~~~~~

The shadow side of my soul, my only identity, the rejection of the ones who persecuted me, came alive. But I kept a wall between myself and white people.

There I was, a small-town girl alone in New York City, in the radical sixties.
I was caught up in "this era of "free love", Marxist revolutionaries, and the Black Power movement.
In my naivety, I even carried around the Little Red Book of Mao Tse-tung. I was swept away by ideology but was not an activist.

I was primed for the militancy of the 60s. When Malcolm X said, "freedom by all means necessary," I said "yes! ". I agreed.

49

At Ann's 11th birthday, I baked a cake for her party with Black Power colors,: red, black and green.

Those words (from years ago when the policeman said, "There is only *one thing worse than a nigger, and that's a nigger-lover")* have carved their groove into my psyche. Ignorance and this hate have been repeated over and over again throughout the years...in all kinds of ways.

**Booker Taliaferro Little**
**This photo was rejected as an album cover because of the sunglasses.**
**He gave it to me.**
**This is the only thing I have that his hands have touched.**

**When I met him**

**My favorite photo cropped from one of his albums**

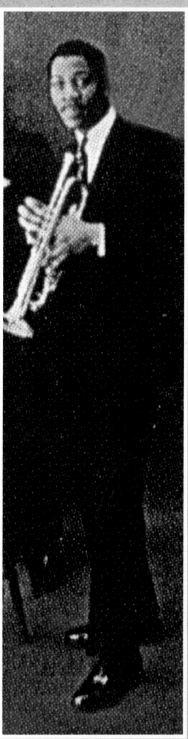

# Chapter Five

SWEET NOTHINGS

Black Power

Baby Boy William

Four years later, while renting a space in a loft on the Lower East Side, I met Michael Ridley, a light-skinned black man, a trumpet player and the younger brother of Larry Ridley, world-renowned bassist and a professor at Rutgers University. It was at a party held by some musicians' wives at a loft apartment in the building where I was temporarily staying. I was still shy and like a child starving for attention.

Michael noticed this and drew me out. We began to see each other every day. After my work at an office, I would pick up Baby Ann from the Puerto Rican babysitter. Michael would meet us and the three of us would take long walks around the city.

After seeing each other for about three months, I willingly laid down with him. And then two weeks later, again. This time, during love-making, I felt a definite "ping". He had opened my womb and, not knowing yet, I had conceived.

After losing Booker, I had lived a celibate life taking care of my daughter. Michael, a shy and quiet man, was the first to show interest in me. Also…he was a trumpet player.

The next month, I did not get my menstrual period and made an appointment with the doctor. After the exam, the doctor said bluntly, "Yep. That's a pregnant uterus".

Taken aback, I left and immediately called Michael from a phone booth on the street.

"Just left the doctor's office. He says I am pregnant".

Michael responded, "What are you trying to *pull*?"

I thought…"*trying to pull*…?" I felt a stab in my heart. Stunned and hurt, I said, "Nothing." And hung up on him.

I did not hear from him again until nine months later…

~~~~~~~~~~~~~~~~~~~

I moved with my four-year old daughter to a sixth-floor walk-up, a tenement on East Houston Street, way downtown in lower Manhattan. I was five months pregnant now when there was a knock at the door. When I opened the door, no one was there. But a threatening note was left, "*I am going to kill you and your nigger baby*".
This went on for a few days. The knock at the door, another note left, then I would hear someone running down the stairs.

I did not call the police because I had a fear of them due to my past experience back home.

So I went to somebody else. I had made friends with some black revolutionaries, writers who belonged to UMBRA, a writer/poets group including David Henderson, who wrote Jimi Hendrix's biography, *S'cuse Me While I Kiss the Sky*; Ishmael Reed and Calvin Herndon, both successful writers; and poets Charles and William Patterson. Some of them joked that I did not seem like other whites and that maybe my mother "had a nigger hidden in the woodpile".

They asked one another about me, "Wonder what Malcolm would think of *her*?" I wore my hair in long braids…maybe they thought I wasn't entirely white…

So I went to them and told them of those threatening notes that were being left at my door.

William Patterson offered to stay with me and try to catch the race hater who was threatening to kill me and my child. For three days and three nights he slept on my sofa, waiting for another knock at the door. Then the knock came; William jumped up from the sofa, ran down the six flights of stairs but the person got away.

It did not happen again.

My identification with Black Power militancy was deep. I would go to Harlem by myself on the subway to hear Malcolm X speak. I admired him. "Dignity Without Compromise," he would say.

~~~~~~~~~~~~~~~~~

I spent those winter months with a growing belly and with my daughter. Ann was four years old now, very bright and independent. I didn't know much how to show physical affection, but she knew I loved her and she was a happy child.

Sometimes there was no heat in the tenement, and we would sit huddled together at the stove to stay warm. One Christmas, a very wealthy friend, Fred Lyman, who admired Booker, sent little Ann and me both red cashmere sweaters from Saks Fifth Avenue! Ann's sweater was trimmed with real fur. Together we huddled at the stove in those red sweaters and had a very, very warm, Merry Christmas!

~~~~~~~~~~~~~~~~~

53

I was five and a half months along with my pregnancy when Cookie Gilchrist showed up. He would occasionally put tracers out to find me. He was a star player with the Buffalo Bills and was in town to play the New York Jets.

After the game, he took me with him, pregnant and all, to the club, Birdland, where trumpter Dizzy Gillespie, was appearing. The host at the door was a black man who was rude and disrespectful to us and looking at us with contempt as we were entering the club. My A-line black dress was meant to disguise my pregnancy.

Dizzy Gillespie realized Cookie Gilchrist was in the house and Cookie was the star of the game that day. Dizzy announced to the audience that the Bills had won and Cookie had scored three touchdowns. There was big applause, and Cookie stood up from the booth and waved to the crowd, enjoying the acclaim.

When he sat back down, I asked, "How could you do that when just a while ago we were treated with such disrespect?"

Cookie answered, "I don't care".

Then Dizzy Gillespie came over and sat in the booth with us. Cookie ate up all the attention. I just sat there, keeping silent throughout.

And after we left the club, he then took me with him to a party in his suite at the Roosevelt Hotel with the other team members.

At the party later that evening, I told Cookie that the baby's father didn't have any contact with me and I considered an abortion. Cookie yelled at me, "Bette Ann, you could kill yourself! You stop that!" When I left, he took a black onyx ring that I had admired off his pinky finger and gave it to me.

Years later, William joined the United States Army and changed his last name to his father's last name, Ridley.

Sometime after his discharge, he contacted Michael and began a relationship with him and an even closer relationship with his famous uncle, Larry Ridley.

When Michael Ridley passed away, there was a huge memorial held for him in New York City. Hundreds of musicians were there.

I urged William who had gotten married and had a son of his own now, to go to the memorial and to take his son, Quinton, with him. They went and were met by many, many musician friends and were included in the eulogy, listed as "son and grandson"...

Today, William is a basketball coach living in New York. He is also a musician and enjoying a great relationship with his Uncle Larry.

**At a loft party the night I met Michael Ridley**

**Me with my son, William.**

**He love to be carried by his mom
and wouldn't take "NO" for an answer**

**Ann at seven years old and William was three**

**Ann and William playing in the sandbox
Thompson Square Park, New York**

**William ready for his first meeting with his father**

**His eleventh birthday party with family and friends**

# Chapter Six

AND SO ON AND SO FORTH

Lower East Side

Baby Girl Dala

With two children now, I moved to Ninth Street and Avenue B in Manhattan. My life was full with music and creativity and many musician friends. Some famous, some on their way to fame. Always they were black; I was afraid of white men.

One day a black writer, an acquaintance, came visiting, and caught me scrubbing the kitchen floor. He stared at me as I was down on my hands and knees.

" Oh no! This is all wrong! This is not what I should be seeing. You should be *arranging flowers!"*

He returned a few days later and brought a gift. A book called *Japanese Flower Arranging.* I still have it.

I wish I could remember that man's name.

~~~~~~~~~~~~~~~~~~~

The old Devil, still looking for ways to destroy, came into my life in the form of a man, offering the illusion of protection - a very good-looking, very articulate man.

My friend, Don Moore, a bass player, and Jimmy Cobb, a sax player, came to visit one day and brought with them Dale Birt Bouggess, Jr.  He was part black, Creole and Cherokee, a chess player, who smoked a pipe, and was a trumpet player who did not play. He introduced himself as "Birt".

He was staying at Don's apartment because he was recently released from a New York prison, freshly clean and sober. A gentleman from a middle-class family in Los Angeles, Birt was extremely intense, but calm and collected. He was classified as an expert in chess tournaments, and occasionally I would run into him in the street carrying a chessboard under his arm. Birt was big and strong, a powerful-looking man.

We developed a brother/sister relationship. He would visit bringing groceries, and romp with the children while I would be in the kitchen cooking. Birt sat at the table with open chess books, studying the chess masters for hours moving the chess pieces around, playing chess with himself.

He showed no interest in sex, and I felt I had a friend. I felt protected by his presence. I thought I had found a gem among the pebbles.

But, after about three months, Birt was back on drugs. That is when the demonic spirit of drugs entered my life. "When the drugs go in, the soul goes out," I thought.

I knew of many men who used heroin and cocaine, and in my ignorance, I saw that kind of high as much "cooler" than getting drunk on alcohol .

Birt once said to me, "The drug… you take your Being from it."

It was years later that I began to see the truth of his words. I understand addicts whose whole being is in pain, because I, too, was in that kind of pain.

~~~~~~~~~~~~~~~~~

Once when Birt was released from Rikers Island Penitentiary, I had clothes waiting for him: a shirt, pants, underwear, and a raincoat. I visited him a couple of times in that prison, going across the river on a barge, leaving him a few dollars.

Sitting together on a bench at the edge of the East River, Birt and I talked about his recent release from prison

"That was the last time. I'm never shooting heroin again", Birt declared.

I believed he meant it, and we began a more intimate relationship and that is when he revealed a long scar on his chest from an icepick attack in Harlem when a drug deal went bad.

Birt was arrested again many times over, always for possession of narcotics. It was easier for me when Birt was in jail, because then I didn't have the stress of not knowing what or when to expect him to come around. I slept better. Out of jail, he would shoot heroin, then rail against eating pork. He had become a Muslim in jail.

Another year went by with our "off again/on again" friendship. There were only rare occasions of sex. Soon after one of those occasions, I realized I was pregnant.

Birt was strung out by then. I ran away from him, children in tow, and moved four times. But he would find us every time. He became possessive, the same kind of possessiveness as Cookie Gilchrist and my father.

Birt knew a "good thing" when he met me. He would say that he was not giving up a "good thing," declaring, "I'll kill a nigga over you". I mistakenly believed that showed how much he cared about me. But it really meant how much Birt did not want to lose his "good thing".

~~~~~~~~~~~~~~~~~

I moved to get away from him for the fifth time to an apartment in Brooklyn on St. John's Place near the Brooklyn Museum. But someone told him where we were now living. He found us and stayed around off and on, in and out of jail, running the streets, chasing the high.

He'd say, "There's no hope without dope".

~~~~~~~~~~~~~~~~~~

At eight and a half months pregnant, my obstetrician called and wanted to admit me to the hospital two weeks before my baby's due date, because I needed intravenous antibiotics due to a leaking heart valve. I made arrangements with a neighbor who owned a child care center in her home, to have Ann and William stay there. I took the subway alone to New York Infirmary in Manhattan, the same hospital where my son was born four years before.

On June 25, I went into labor and gave birth for the third time. Alone.

Two days later, Dale Birt Bouggess Jr. came to the hospital. It was *1:00 AM*, and I could hear him from my hospital room making a ruckus in the hallway, telling the nurses, "I want to see my baby." He did not yet know if it was a boy or girl. Everyone had thought I was carrying a boy, and Birt wanted a boy whom he would name Dale Birt Bouggess, the Third.

The day before I was discharged, he signed paternity papers for his daughter.

I had given my baby girl the name Dala.

I hoped beyond hope that Birt would clean up and be a good father.

~~~~~~~~~~~~~~~~~~

Birt was a man with no credentials…..and I secretly admired this and identified with it, because I had none either.

He only listened to modern progressive music, the likes of Thelonious Monk, Miles Davis, and John Coltrane.  I enjoyed that music also. Birt would not listen to Rhythm & Blues.

One day I asked, "Why?".

He answered, "They're always cryin', moanin', or bitchin' about some woman…",

~~~~~~~~~~~

A musician friend thought that Birt was "the glibbest man he ever met."

Some BIRT-ISMS:

*What is, is.*

*And so on and so forth.*

*Is that right?*

*Sure you know.*

*Sure you're right.*

*Quiet as it's kept.*

*Yet and still*

*All well and good.*

*Y' understand?*

Birt's explanation of politics was "It's *all* economics. Giant con."

**Me and Dale Birt Bouggess, Jr. sitting in Tomkins Square Park on the lower East Side of Manhattan, pontificating on the "coming Black Revolution"**

**Prospect Park with Baby Dala just home from the hospital**

**Dala at five years old,
thrilled with her Schwinn bike from her daddy**

Ah, Brooklyn! Dala (age three) and Mommy out for a stroll in our neighborhood

# Chapter Seven

SHE BURNS COAL

California

Los Angeles Houses


With three children now, I left New York for Los Angeles when the kids were eleven, seven and two years old. One more time, I wanted to get away from Birt, so I accepted an invitation from my brother to come to Los Angeles, share a house with him, and take care of his two-year-old child whose mother had left.

It took me three months to sell everything and use the money for airfare, ship our mattresses, our clothes, and a few personal treasures. When in LA, I built our beds using sheets of plywood and 4x4 blocks for the legs.

After about six months living with my brother, he decided to get his own place, so I had to find an apartment, and it was a challenge with three kids and no job.

I found work at many office jobs, moving several times to different apartments.

The day after I left New York, Birt was arrested for possession of narcotics and sentenced to one year in prison.

The day after his release, he flew to Los Angeles where his relatives were living. His mother, writing to him in jail, revealed to him that I and the children had moved to an apartment on Braddock Drive in a section of Los Angles called Culver City.

Freshly clean and sober again, he wanted to stay with us. He had been on a work program in prison and arrived with $1000 in his pocket. He visited us and bought Schwinn bikes for all three of the kids, the only time he ever contributed that way.

~~~~~~~~~~~~~~~~~

Although I had been accused of wishing and hoping for what seemed very unlikely, I thought "maybe" this time Birt would stay off drugs and be a father to the children.

The old "potential freak" arose in me again.

I let him in and he was back in my life.

I met his mother, step-father, and the families of his four sisters and their children. We socialized with them on many holidays and other family gatherings. Some of his relatives lived in integrated middle-class neighborhoods, and some in black upper-class areas. One of his aunts lived on a street near the home of singer, Ray Charles. They were a close-knit, loving, Christian family,

Birt was the exception..

~~~~~~~~~~~~~~~~~

One afternoon, I began talking…pouring out streams of consciousness for hours, which was very uncharacteristic of me.

Apparently, I was having some kind of "freak-out".

I heard someone saying, "Take her to the hospital, man".

Birt said, "No. She just needs to be held". And he did just that for what seemed hours. Even though our relationship was devoid of any affection, holding me for that long a time calmed me down. I will always remember he did that for me.

66

Within only two weeks of Birt's return, while driving to the grocery store, he slid through a stop-sign. The police stopped him, ran a check and found an old bench warrant from many years ago, and he was taken to jail.

My sister's husband, John Ellena, an attorney, represented him in court pro bono. He had met Birt back in New York, enjoyed playing chess with him, and they both were Navy veterans. Pleading "family relation", all charges were dropped.

~~~~~~~~~~~~~~~~

Cookie Gilchrist keeping a tracer on me, showed up at various places every now and then just to check on how I was doing. He never failed to bring a "drop-dead" gorgeous woman with him.

Birt showed up on one of those same days. Cookie and Birt met and talked together. They seemed to enjoy one another. I did not join the conversation. I was still the quiet one and hardly talked at all, stayed in the background, and kept to myself.

Eventually, Birt went back on drugs again, and was back on the streets.

~~~~~~~~~~~~~~~~

One day I decided to take my brother's suggestion and attempt to buy a house. One of Birt's sisters owned a small four-room house that she wanted to sell. It was located in an all-black, working-class neighborhood on Hillcrest Drive in the Crenshaw district. There was an avocado tree in the front yard and a lemon tree in the back yard.

I could get a GI bank loan if I was married to Birt, who was a veteran from the Navy.

I went looking for him in the streets, found him, and told him I wanted to get a marriage license so that I could get a VA guaranteed loan to buy a house for the children. Birt agreed to do it.

The VA appraised the house for the full asking price of $30,000. Therefore, I only needed closing costs of $900, which I charged on my Bank of America credit card.

I repaired, painted and fixed the house up, hung a basketball net on the garage door where Birt taught William basketball fundamentals, and made some improvements with every paycheck;

Two years later I sold it for $59,500. This enabled me to buy an eight-room, four-bedroom house off Angelus Vista in an integrated, middle-class area. The house included a three-car garage, a lanai, French doors that opened out from the master bedroom to a Japanese garden, and a formal dining room - chandelier and all. Since Birt was on the record as "Joint Tenant" and part owner, he was legally living there, too. He would come in for a few hours, every few days, then leave for the streets again.

Within six months, I had to flee from Birt once more

It was early Saturday. I was in the living room, still in my robe, reading the morning paper. Dala was playing on the floor, William was still asleep and Ann had gone to a friend's house for a sleepover.

Birt showed up. For a long time now, our relationship had not been sexual. He was obviously very high and made unusual advances toward me.

I said, "No! What do you think you are you doing? No!"

Birt went into the kitchen.  Then came out and walked through the dining-room toward me with a butcher knife in his hand. He looked crazed, his hair standing up like Don King's.

"What are you doing?  Give me that!" I said.

I snatched the knife out of his hand and walked through the dining room to the kitchen, and threw the knife back into the drawer.

In a few minutes, he came toward me again with the knife.  I had never seen him as wasted as this, and I knew then I had to get away.

I grabbed Dala who was playing on the living-room floor, and ran out the front door.  My car was in the driveway and we took off.

As I was backing out, there was Birt standing in the yard in his robe. He was slashing his wrists with the butcher knife. I fled to the house of a relative of Birt's, Eugene, who lived nearby.  Hearing what was going on, he had us sit down in his kitchen while he went off to check on Birt.

When he reached my house, Birt was gone.

I went back to get my son who had been sleeping through it all, and we fled to my parents' home as they had moved to Los Angeles.  I needed to be there until I could find a place to live. Understandably, they were not happy with this, but they felt they had no choice but to allow us to stay.

After two weeks, I went back to my house and there were signs that Birt was still living there. I found the place empty. He had sold everything except some large pieces of furniture.

I put the house up for sale, but he was still in the house and would not allow the realtor to show it.

The real estate agent, a black women, was curious about my relationship with Birt. She commented that she had never seen such a mismatch before and said she didn't mean racial differences.

I explained that he was an addict, and with that she nonchalantly said, "You are going to have to shoot him." She shared with me that she also had to shoot an abusive boyfriend who would not leave her alone.

Since I was not going to shoot anyone, and to get Birt out of the house to enable her to show it to potential buyers, she suggested and I agreed to offer him $4000 from escrow if he would sign the house over to me with a Quit Claim Deed. He signed it, quickly took the money, and was gone.

I rented an apartment, but the mortgage plus my apartment rent was more than I could keep up. The house had to be sold, but the vultures got it from me for next to nothing.

After losing that second house that I had worked to achieve, you'd think I would be devastated. I felt deserted as my pleas to both sides of family for financial help were ignored.

I went on to the next thing to survive.

~~~~~~~~~~~~~~~~~~~~

A few years later, I was summoned to the Emergency room of University of California Los Angeles Hospital. Birt was there out of his mind and high on drugs. Apparently he was pacing up and down and "preaching".

70

When I arrived, the doctor asked me, "Is he a very religious man?" I answered, "No. But his mother was a preacher".

Later, a bill came to me from the hospital for $800. I was legally Birt's wife and responsible for his debts.

Over the next few years, I moved again to various apartments. The first move after losing the house was to an apartment in the Mar Vista area not far from the beach. Three months after we moved in, the owner wanted to sell it as a condo for $100,000 which I clearly couldn't afford to buy, so we had to move again. I found an apartment in a not-so-great neighborhood near Kaiser Hospital and after a few months living there, we had a break-in. The burglary happened in the daytime while I was at work.

I received a phone call from Birt who had gotten my number from someone he knew at the phone company.

I answered and told him , "Birt, we are divorced. I had gone to court and had paid my brother-in-law, the attorney, $300."

"You just threw away $300 because I don't care what any white man says. You are still my wife." This was Birt's response.

~~~~~~~~~~~~~~~~

I moved out of that neighborhood and rented a very nice condo in Inglewood.

Things were settling down.

William was thinking of joining the Army, and that same year Ann got married. She had a beautiful church wedding, white gown, bridesmaids and all.

William "gave the bride away".

By the end of the year, I became a grandmother.

Ann named my first grandson, Booker, after his grandfather.

~~~~~~~~~~~~~~~~

One afternoon, I was driving to San Fernando Valley to visit a friend. I pulled up to the building about 8:30 in the evening. While I was getting out of my car, I reached back in for my handbag and felt something pointed right in the middle of my back.

I turned around and heard "Give me the keys, bitch!".

There were two men standing there, one with a gun pointed straight at my chest. The other grabbed my handbag off my shoulder. They were neatly dressed in black sweaters and slacks. The one with the gun had a dark-skinned complexion, and the other was light-skinned.

I thought, *"Give me the keys bitch?... they are taking my car!"*.

I had just finished four years worth of payments on the car and I had just received the pink owner's papers.

*"Give me the keys, bitch"*, one of the men yelled again.

I stared into the eyes of the one holding the gun on me and then I looked back down to the gun.

I thought, *"Is that a real gun?*

I looked back and forth into his eyes and back down to the gun so many times that the other man got nervous and said "Come on, man!" He went around to the passenger side of the car.

I kept thinking, *"This is it. This is how my life is going to end. They got my handbag! Now I have no ID... I'm going to be in the gutter... a Jane Doe... this is how my life is ending ..."*

72

Unspeakable rage welled up out of me from the pit of my bowels.

I said, *"Here!"*

And slammed the keys into his hand.

It took him by surprise. The other man was urging, "Come on, man!" and with that, the one with the gun turned, and I scooted back and ducked down behind the back of the car.

They got into the car and drove away. I believe that the way I responded to them saved my life. If I had begged them and pleaded "please don't hurt me, don't hurt me , pul-lease", I think I probably would have been shot.

Three days later, the police found my car in the gang-ridden Nickerson projects in Watts. Stripped, trunk crowbarred, wheels gone, and it was sitting on blocks. Gang graffiti all over it.

I was working at Santa Monica/Malibu Unified School District at this time, and my auto insurance eventually paid for all the repairs.

~~~~~~~~~~~~~~~~~

Birt was now living on Skid Row in downtown Los Angeles.

He showed up at our daughter's Sweet Sixteen party. When the party was over, he refused to leave and pleaded that he wanted to stay.

I gave him an ultimatum. "Go to Narcotics Anonymous every day with a Sponsor". Birt agreed to it.

I agreed to let him stay….because he was Dala's daddy.

Some of the men from NA told me later that when Birt spoke at meetings, you could hear a pin drop.

Three days before getting his three-month "chip'" for sobriety, I left him sitting at the kitchen table, his trumpet in his hand, and I went off to work.

When I came home eight hours later, he was still sitting at the table, holding his trumpet in hand, finishing off a big bottle of whisky.

I said, "Birt, you have to go."

He ignored me.

I called his Sponsor, who came right over with two other men and after talking with him, escorted him out.

Birt called to me, "I'm not going to make it...", as the men walked with him past an open window.

He ended up back downtown on Skid Row where he collapsed in the street and was taken to a VA hospital since he had been in the Navy.

I got the call from the VA.

He had a massive stroke and stayed there for four months.

I visited often and considered taking care of him, but he was in such bad shape that the doctors said he was like a young child and would need constant supervision.

He had to be placed in a nursing home. They sent him to an awful one in a dangerous neighborhood. I objected to visiting him there and insisted that he be taken to one nearby my home. I had to fight the authorities, but when I informed them that his relatives had given up on him for all intents and purposes, and I most likely would be the only one to visit him, they agreed.

He was transferred to a suitable one that I found in Santa Monica. I would visit and take him out sometime for coffee and doughnuts. One day I took Birt to Century

City to see the movie, *Round Midnight*, about a musician who also struggled with drug addiction. During the film, I watched Birt as he smiled throughout the movie. He had the mentality of a six-year old now caused by years of drug use and a series of small strokes. The doctors gave him less than a year to live.

He survived in that place for eleven years.

And later, some of his siblings did visit.

At his funeral, we were all there.

~~~~~~~~~~~~~~~~~

While working at Santa Monica/Malibu Unified School District, I began to have panic attacks. They came out of nowhere. I finally went to a male psychologist who seemed to be only interested in the sex with black men. On the third session, I walked out.

The panic attacks continued. A doctor prescribed Valium, "Mother's Little Helper". After a few of those blue pills, I felt nothing. No more anxiety. I thought, "Great!, This does for me what I had to do for myself, shut everything off; nothing would bother me".

I finally found a female psychotherapist, Jan Johnson at Open Counseling Center in Culver City, a woman ten years younger than I, who basically re-parented me.

She said to me after hearing my experiences, "Don't even try to expect anyone to understand you. Unless they know your history, no one will."

I continued counseling with her for nine straight years. She encouraged me to attend the 12-step meetings but, at first, I was reluctant to go.

Repression of something that was horribly wrong finally began to break through to my consciousness... signs of paradoxes, conflicts, and contradictions .

During this period, I had an out-of-body experience.

As I was napping one afternoon, I felt my spirit separate from my body and I found myself up in the corner of the ceiling watching myself as I slept. It took every bit of my strength to pull myself down from the ceiling back into my body.

Who knows? Did I temporarily die? Or could it have been the medication?

~~~~~~~~~~~~~~~~~~~

One night out to a club with my sister, someone had sent Martini's to our table and without thinking, I drank them, forgetting that I had taken Valium earlier. I blacked out, and was taken by ambulance to a hospital nearby.

It took nine days to be detoxed in the hospital. When I was discharged, I began to attend Narcotics Anonymous 12-step meetings.

At one of these meetings during a break, I was in line with others to get coffee.

I overheard two men speaking about me. One white and the other Latino.

"Look at her... she looks interesting. How about her?"

His friend replied , "*Not* her man... *not her* ! You don't want anything to do with her."

The other man replies, "Why? why not?"

His friend replied, " She *burns coal*, man. She *burns coal*!"

I immediately knew what they meant. They thought that I lusted after black men.

Once white men saw my brown babies, they did not want anything to do with me and they didn't want to "go there".

But, I was afraid of white men anyway.  Their contempt for me caused a feeling that stayed with me for many years to come.  I thought that the white man was *afraid* of black men.  Also, white men bought the *myth* that black men are sexually superior.

~~~~~~~~~~~~~~~~~~~

After losing the house, I saw that some blacks were as prejudiced as some whites.  I had believed that they would not do what the whites had done to me.  But some did.

I had buried my feelings to the point that I felt nothing. Most of my energy was going into trying to stay invisible, as I did for many years

77

**This is the only photo with all three of my children.
Our last week in New York before leaving for Los Angeles**

**Preparing the Thanksgiving Turkey**

At work as Betty Bouggess at
Santa Monica/Malibu School District

Our first house on Hilcrest Drive, Los Angeles.
The black, blue-collar neighborhood where everyone took
such good care of their surroundings.

**Dale (Birt) returning to LA reuniting with his sisters:
(Left To Right) Barbara, Janice, Carolyn, Martha Ann
Los Angeles, California**

# Chapter Eight

ESTHER AND ME

The Richards Sisters

We Two

As kids, Esther and I were always singing around the house.  Anything I sang…
there would be my little sister harmonizing with me.  Our music together seemed to
have a life of its own.

As teens in Pennsylvania, we continued to sing together around the house.  We
listened to my collection of records and sang along with the musicians on the
recordings. We learned the beautiful ballad, *We Two*, from a J.J. Johnson/Kai Winding
recording, and Esther could sing the harmony just perfectly.

We signed a recording contract with Laurie Records, and the company wanted
us to be the female answer to the Everly Brothers. My sister and I were against this, but
it was part of the deal. We recorded a song called "Kissin' Just to Be Kissin'" which was
given the 'pick to click' and aired on a Pittsburgh radio station. They played it for a week.

Nothing came of it and the song went nowhere.

~~~~~~~~~~~~~~~~

When I had to leave home for New York City, Esther eventually followed, and
then my brother, all of us staying with Bernice on West 84th Street.  When Ann was still
a tiny baby, all of us moved to 101st Street and Broadway. Then, we had to get out of
there when the Manager learned there were four of us in a one-bedroom apartment.  My
brother Dan found a place on 8th Street and Avenue D on the Lower East side which
was roach-infested, so we stayed there only a few months.

He then went back to Pennsylvania, and Esther and I moved into the Lanseer Hotel on 51st Street and Broadway around the corner from the club, Birdland.

My sister and I began singing around town, and I would take my baby wrapped in her blanket to auditions and rehearsals.

Booker visited the Lanseer Hotel often. He came into the kitchen once to meet my sister. She told me she was in awe when he talked to her.

Esther commented, "I knew he could understand without words."

~~~~~~~~~~~~~~~~~

I carried baby Ann to rehearsals, to auditions, and parties, wrapped in her pink blanket while my sister and I made our try at a singing career. During this time, I sewed tan corduroy coats for both of us, made from an idea in *Vogue* magazine. I cut out the pattern from a piece of newspaper.

Rehearsals at the Brill Building in Manhattan were common, and we focused on landing another record deal.

We auditioned once at Columbia Records for Clyde Otis. He liked what he heard and assigned us to a rehearsal pianist there. He said, "When white girls can swing, they can make it".

Another audition was held at the Bitter End Cafe in Greenwich Village. We were dressed casually in blue jeans and I wore my hair in long braids. They were impressed with our sound and booked us to perform the very next week. We were excited and we practiced all week with our own guitarist at the time, John Popalia.

The day of the performance, we took the advice of a friend who thought we should dress alike in party dresses and lose my long braids. We did not like that idea, but we caved in to this suggestion.

The place was packed.

But since we were not true to ourselves, not relaxed, we did not go over as we did at the audition the week before. This also went nowhere.

Later, we signed with a manager, Nick Quesado, who got us a demo recording audition at RCA Studios. While recording in Studio A, Harry Belafonte was recording in Studio B and on break, he came in to check us out and we were told he seemed to like what he heard.

Esther and I had one of our many arguments right before the recording session and we faced away from each while we sang. We had these fights when one or the other couldn't get her way.

When the "powers that be'" heard our demo, their decision was "They're not hungry enough."

Esther was very outgoing socially, but always experienced nervous stage fright just before we were ready to perform. I would tell her as big sis to little sis, "Just watch me."

I was the opposite. I had all the confidence performing especially if I could depend on the accompanying musicians to know our "style". But socially, I was extremely reserved and rarely at ease.

Another time our brother paid $400 for music arrangements by Slide Hampton, a highly respected musical arranger. We lost them in our many moves, never to be found.

Our singing "career" came to a halt when my sister met a wonderful man, got married, and moved to Los Angeles. Over the next few years, she had four children.

Now I had three, and I later moved out to Los Angeles with my children as well.

~~~~~~~

With our kids older, Esther and I resumed our singing together, this time in Los Angeles with blues musician Leon Blue and his Blues Band. We were booked all around town, Hollywood, and down the coast. We sang often at a club called *Peanuts* on Santa Monica Boulevard in the back room called the "VIP Room" and at *Oscars,* an English pub at 8210 Sunset Boulevard, West Hollywood.,

One night after our set, we returned to our table and two men came and joined us. They introduced themselves as Slash and Axl. At that time my sister and I had no knowledge of hard rock or heavy metal and so therefore, we did not realize we were talking to Guns & Roses! They asked us where we were from, and how long we had been singing.

Slash gave me his phone number, which I kept for many years but never got around to calling.

One night Esther and I were invited to sing at *B B King's Club* in Universal City. When we sang our signature song, *Sorry, Baby*, a slow blues, the whole room went silent.

Then the crowd broke out with applause and loud cheers. We were a hit. The musicians told us that we could probably be an opening act for a big name.

We were asked for our "press kit". But we didn't have a "press kit" nor knowledge of one. We had no management, and so another opportunity went nowhere.

~~~~~~~

*Harvelle's*, a club on the Third Street Promenade in Santa Monica, was a place where all kinds of musicians would gather and jam after coming off the road from their tours. Esther and I sang there many nights. We loved it because one never knew what great musicians might come through that door and then we would get to jam with them, thrilled to have that kind of accompaniment.

One night, the place was packed, and as we came down from the bandstand and sat down at our table, I noticed that someone had taken my seat because there was a beautiful leather jacket hanging on the back of my chair. The owner of the jacket came over and introduced himself as one of the members of Jefferson Airplane.

Later, when I was leaving, he put the jacket around me and said, "It's yours." We chatted, he asked me where I lived, and I gave him my phone number.

A couple of days later, he sent me two dozen roses with a note saying there was a "cracker jack" surprise in the flowers. It was a silver and turquoise Indian ring. I never learned his name and I never heard from him again.

Over the years I met many musicians who showed some interest in me but I was still in my own world and never really responded.

~~~~~~~~~~~~~~~~~~

Time passed.  Esther and I would get together and go out to clubs and sing every now and them.

We recorded an album of eight songs of mixed styles, including two of our originals. We called the album "In the Garage" which is where we recorded it with one musician playing all parts on a synthesizer. One of the originals was *Sorry Baby*, our signature song, and the other, *Remember the Last Time* which I wrote for a loved one who was caught up in a cycle of abuse.  I later wrote a handbook of the same name to accompany the song.

We co-wrote a beautiful ballad inspired from the lyrics of a poem we saw in the newspaper. The notations were graciously written out for us by my very dear friend, a magnificent pianist, John Hicks, who was playing at the Lighthouse in Hermosa Beach at the time along with trumpeter Lee Morgan's group. The song is called *Please Keep Loving Me* which we never got around to recording.

Sometimes when we would sing country songs, Esther and I jokingly called each other "Willa and Waylette", a female version of country singers, Willie Nelson and Waylan Jennings,  and we'd get into arguments about who would be Wayla and who would be Willette.  When we sang Rhythm and Blues, we became "Odella and Nadine".

~~~~~~~~~~~~~~~~~~~

I was never happier than when I was singing with my sister.

Other than singing together, Esther and I lived opposite lives.

She was married to a successful attorney, John Ellena. They lived a bourgeois life in the white suburbs of West Covina in the eastern section of San Gabriel Valley.

I lived with my kids in mostly black or integrated areas and hung out only with black musicians, artists, and writers.

Esther and I clashed about a lot of things, but nobody could make us laugh as hard as we did with one another.

We had a unique sound and style together.

And it was pure joy…especially when we received a compliment from the musicians who said, "you sounded good!"

*Two sisters on the West Coast, aware that music was their life force, singing energizing, sometimes heartbreaking lyrics and melody.*

*Two sisters in New York City hanging out with the greats of jazz and soul, singing together, gospel-country-blues.*

*Two little sisters in rural Pennsylvania sitting on the bank of Bull Creek, kicking their feet in the water as they sang.*

*"…just doing what we love to do…"*

My relationship itself with Esther, though, was a *folie 'a deux. (shared madness)*

**Teaching my little sister how to play 1-2-3 O'Leary**

**Esther and I the night she arrived in Los Angeles**

# Bette & Esther

SIGN RECORDING CONTRACT — The Richard Sisters, Betty Ann and Esther, daughters of Mr. and Mrs. Gerald Richards, Cedar St., Tarentum, have signed a three-year contract and have cut their first record. The girls, who have composed nine songs of their own, will make their records on the Laurie label. Just released is their first venture into the recording field, "All I Have to Do Is Dream," with "Kissin' Just To Kissin'" on the flip side. They have lived Prospect Heights, Brooklyn, for two years with their brother, Daniel, who is employ by a Wall Street brokerage firm. During brief visit home this weekend, the you women will visit district radio stations sing at a record hop. They attended Tar tum and Har-Brack schools.

## Esther & Bette
## in earlier times

*When you accepted him back,*

*you forgot how he hurt you.*

*Remembering* could save your life...

# REMEMBER the LAST TIME

Bette Ann Richards is the author of
several previous works.

# REMEMBER
# THE
# LAST TIME

### Becoming Aware of the
### Cycle of Abuse

When you accepted him back,
did you forget?

*Remembering*

could save your life.

MUSIC CD INSIDE

# B. A. Richards

## 2 versions of a small handbook

# Chapter Nine

STEPPING OUT

Bette's Blues

Singing Alone


With my children all grown up and living in other parts of the country,  I finally had enough of office jobs.  I resigned from the Santa Monica/Malibu School District where I worked for nine years.  I withdrew all my retirement money and moved to Venice Beach at Breeze Avenue, a walk-street; to Rose Avenue; and to Main Street where a replica of a giant clown stood at the corner; then across the border line to Barnard Way in Santa Monica.  I lived on that money for two years.

During that time, I took classes (Science of Mind) with Michael Beckwith of Agape International Spiritual Center, and also attended 12-step program meetings in Al-Anon for Families. I did not set foot in a church.

When the money ran out, I continued at various office manager jobs in small companies and would work there for a few months to gather enough money to get by, and then quit.  I did this for several years, never staying at one office longer than necessary.

It was getting clearer as to what I wanted, what I liked, and what I didn't like. I attended Assertiveness Training classes to practice expressing myself instead of holding back.

Singing with my sister was on again/off again. We went back to work in various blues clubs and festivals usually getting gigs with the blues pianist, Leon Blue and His Blues Band.

While working at a club in Hollywood one night, Esther did not show up.

So I sang without my sister for the first time.

There was a female producer present who liked my style. She proposed bankrolling an album using her lyrics for which Leon Blue and I would write the music. Because of the love and respect of the musicians I knew, I was able to recruit some of the best for this recording session held at Clear Lake Audio on Burbank Blvd. in North Hollywood.

James Gadson on drums, led the session. He had been recorded on over 300 Mo-Town hits; Kevin Moore on guitar, later known as Grammy-winner Keb Mo; Michael Smith on piano who worked with Natalie Cole; and Jerry Johnson on bass, said to have toured with Crosby, Stills and Nash; and John D. Stephens, arranger for many famous artists too numerous to name.

These were great musicians, top of the line, and I was in seventh heaven having them accompany me.

I had no management, and one of the musicians urged me to ask the producer for a percentage of the publishing. The producer declined. After laying all the music tracks, and I sang what is called "scratch vocals" with the musicians as they laid their tracks, I asked her once again for a piece of the publishing. She did not want to hear it. After my third plea, the producer then threw me off the session and got someone else to finish the vocals.

I heard later that she hired another singer to record with my arrangements. Just like that, I was left out.

This whole encounter was a great disillusionment to me because I believed that at least two of those songs were great. I am not aware if that producer ever gained anything using my music.

All I have from this session is a recording of a rough mix of my vocals I sang while the musicians laid their music tracks.

I call it Bette's Blues.

~~~~~~~~~~~~~~~~~~

While living at Rose Ave in Venice Beach, Larry Davis, a great black blues singer/guitarist, would sometimes sit in and sing with me at *Oscars* on Santa Monica Boulevard in Hollywood. He thought my sound belonged in Memphis, Tennessee, where he was planning to take his group on his band bus to do some recordings. He invited me to go along. He said he'd be in touch.

I waited to hear from him for about two months and didn't get any call, so I decided to call him.

A woman answered. I told her who I was and that Larry had invited me to go to Memphis with his band.

Her reply…"Larry passed away a month ago."

Needless to say, I was shocked and saddened by the loss of a great bluesman, a dear friend, and a shattered dream.

~~~~~~~~~~~~~~~~~~~

Another admirer of my singing was Richard Bach (not the writer), a tall, good-looking blond man who heard me singing in a small country/western bar. We hit it off and began seeing each other. He liked my singing and told me he "heard angels when I sang".

One night when he did not show up, I learned Richard was killed by his ex-girlfriend. They got into an argument and she had been drinking. She left the club in anger, and when backing her car up to leave, did not realize he was in the parking lot. Richard's ex hit him, and dragged him for two blocks underneath her car, killing him.

This was a beautiful, soulful, strong, man, who would often say to me, "Bette, you are denying the world *if you do not sing.*"

Richard was the first white man that I allowed any closeness.

The second was a Jewish man, Ed Hochstein. When we met, he had already made plans to leave the United States and move to Israel. He invited me with my children to live with him on Kibbutz Barkai on the Jordan border.

I responded to him because he was a man with a very poetic soul, and it was unusual for me to be wanted in that way.

I declined his offer. I would not go on my own. I needed to have him come and take me away.

But that fear of white men was beginning to fade.

~~~~~~~~~~~~~~~~~~~

I continued to take classes at Santa Monica College. I completed a two-day workshop for Violence Against Women which featured my song, *Remember the Last Time*. I sang it on campus, also featuring my handbook with the same title.

I was recommended for a scholarship.

I thought I'd try for a degree in Engineering and Design (I had always admired architects and considered becoming one), but the scholarship was given to another. The reason? Not enough "points".

I had points for being a woman…

Had points for having little money…

Had points for being the first in my family to earn a degree…

But I did not get the scholarship because being *white* did not grant me enough points. Feeling angry and dejected, I refused to take my last final exam. I dropped out.

Some years later, I received a bill for that class from the Department of Treasury for a few thousand dollars, as it had been funded by a government Pell Grant.

**5 Rose Avenue, Venice Beach, CA**

**I dropped out of society for several years and lived here on the sixth floor.**

When I made the "career" decision to "go it alone"
Clown Building, Main Street, Venice, California
Courtesy of photographer Philip Ghee

**Happiest after returning from a gig with some great musicians.**

**Rushing to get ready**

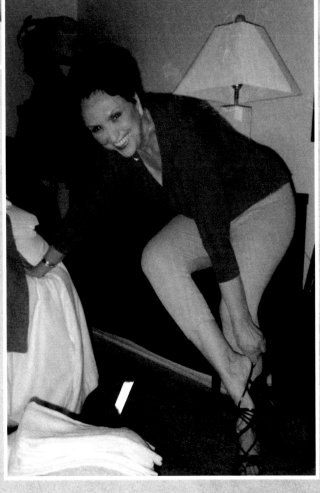

# Chapter Ten

COLLAGES OF SHAME

A Mosaic of Musings and Poems

### *Venice Beach in the morning*

*If you stay down there long enough, you see them all. Dope fiends, crack smokers, crazies. Knew just about every kind. Weak sisters i called them. Now and an occasional then, one would still have some life left in him - a flash of brightness still in his eyes. These, i immediately got a "crush" on. i would go so long without seeing that light. Then, when i did, it would hit my heart. i would see the men in the morning - on the boardwalk - lying on the beach - crippled from the war - i watch them from a distance - after the body then the crippled soul - but the soul does not need legs to fly - i am the same - do they lie there on the beach, alone, dreaming of another time? - or are they all the way deadened, numbed by their pain? - my instincts are always to go to them - to ask them to go home with me - to combine our misery? - no harmony there they are full of wine. It is not rescuing i want to do with them - what is it - to meet - to touch -*

*he is lying in the sand - i want to go over and look at his face - i wonder if he is too drunk - there is a bottle propped up in the sand - crutches lay by his side*

~~~~~~~

*One man was my own disappointment - he was a black artist expressing life - a gift to me to come into my experience - and yet i could not feel myself - he presented an unreal image - where does it come from? - is it the saboteur? - "are you cold?" he*

*asked- "I sleep in a garage", he said with light contempt - i thought…you are good ..you*

*are a good man - i remember these same words told to me - "you are good. you are a*

*good woman" - so what? how did that make him feel? - where is the thing that throws*

*me out of whack? lack of confidence? - i say, "i don't like my body" hoping i will hear*

*"Your body is beautiful" - instead, he says, "if you don't like your body, do something*

*about it!" - not the answer I wanted.*

~~~~~~

*I would stare at couples walking together, always noticing the women who wore*

*diamond ring wedding sets….marveled at their staying together for all those years*

*….could not imagine how much the man loved her to put those rings on her fingers*

*for life….wondered but could not imagine how that felt…..*

~~~~~~

While living in Apartment 59 at Rose Avenue, a six-story, low-income building on Venice Beach, my neighbor, Sam Birnkrant, a retired playwright, lived next door in Apt. 60. He was Jewish and quite older than I was, and I often ran errands for him. I would drive him to North Hollywood and watch young actors perform his plays, and occasionally to the Jewish cemetery where his mother was buried. He would stand in front of the burial wall and talk to his mother for hours while I waited.

Sam never married, and was full of stories. He claimed to have walked the beach with the likes of Marilyn Monroe and other actresses.

His neighbor, an old man, kept asking Sam to commit suicide together with him. The man was good-looking and probably even handsome when he was younger.

Sam would tell me about this guy wanting to die together, and Sam would always have an eerie smile on his face.

Some years later after I had moved away, Goldman Sachs had to track me down because Sam, who had died in a nursing home, had left me a substantial sum of money! Sam had once said to me, gently placing his hand on my shoulder, "You are the only person I know who has been *stoned* because of going against society's mores." I believe I was the only non-Jewish person listed in his Last Will and Testament.

And I didn't stop crying for four days.


### Continuing with Jan Johnson, my therapist...

Therapist:    The  entire first year of our sessions, you never uttered the word, "I".

Me:   I do not believe I have low "self-esteem". I do believe I am good enough, sometimes I even excel. But, ultimately… rejection.

Therapist:  Your identity is that of a black male, a musician, or a drug addict.

Me:     I am not a "Southern White Woman"….never been put on anybody's pedestal. Measured my strength by how much bad treatment I withstood. "Successful" thoughts never entered my mind. Living on a level of survival in shadows of desperation. Did not pay attention to any powers that I might have.

*Nights: having those trapped dreams again…..*

*Is there any compassion for white victims?  My experience did not show any.*

*No way out - unable to move -  unable to scream*

*Their unspoken words are "You don't need anything….die, nigger lover…die.*

FACETS OF MY MIND:

( innocent      abandoned      ugly duckling      do not fit anywhere)

Sadie Saboteur      works 4 u but not 4 me

Carrie Caretaker    mother

Sister Sally        big older sis

Betty Boop          singer

Leona Lonely        lost child

Ann Analyzer        brainiac

Artesia Artist      spatial genius

Mary Mother         protector of brown babies

~~~~~~~~

I found books to help me understand how to be a good mother because I did not
have a clue beyond taking care of my babies' basic needs (which I did with hyper-
vigilance).  The books were *How Children Succeed* and *How Children Fail* by John Holt.

~~~~~~~~~~~~~~~~~~

POEM  given to me by Christa Gerhard July 12, 1991

To Dear Bette - Who also knows "the pain that tears the heart", and is transcending it.

## UNBELONGING

*The pain of Unbelonging*

*Is pain that tears the heart*

*With nothing we can call our own*

*We don't know where to start*

*Stripped of person, place and thing*

*We're naked in the wind*

*Unaware of how it happened*

*Where or how we've sinned!*

*Fear won't ease its cruel grip*

*As anguish shrieks aloud*

*Unbelonging is the curse*

*…we vanish in the crowd*


POEM  by my cousin, Frank Betush (after my gift to him of a dreamcatcher)

Thank you, cuz.

*Deep in winter's discontent*

*A planet at solstice pirouettes*

*Whilst feathered leather, web-in-hoop*

*By Ancient's charm my dreams kept clear*

97

POEM  by Bernice Miller

To Ophilia  (the name given to me by my friend, the woman with whom my mother arranged to send me away to New York)

*She had a dance with anger last night*

*As it led her into its deadly trap*

*Suffering in silence because no one could feel her pain*

*Holding back the tears*

*Overshadowing the gentle falling rain*

*She was lost to the world*

*Escaping into madness*

*Finding yesterday not measuring her dance steps*

*to her music inside.*

Love, from Peleni Penally (Bernice's pen name)

Another POEM by Bernice who spoke for me at times

*Jesus, My Lord, My Savior*

*I lie there in the storm of life*

*could not laugh*

*could not cry*

*no meaning*

*no purpose*

*You called my name and whispered I Love You*

*and, I sang out! Jesus my Lord My Savior*

*With grace I praise your name*

*You held my hand and led me in from the rain*

*I saw the laughter in the faces of children*

*and remembered it was You who put it there*

*and when the tears came,*

*You were there to embrace me*

*so not to more despair*

*You chose my angels for your celestial choir*

*My Jesus My Lord My Savior*

*Praising Your name, you gave me purpose*

*I will carry my cross*

*Singing and praising*

*praising Your name*

POEM  by Bette Richards

THE PREDATOR AND THE PREY

*IT*

*was a lie.*

99

*He*

*"That's what's wrong with you...*

*You won't let anyone love you...*

*Just let me love you..."*

*SHE*

*believed him.*

*She always felt the opposite.*

*No one knew her*

*let alone loved her.*

*BUT*

*he was telling her*

*to receive his love.*

*Her heart opened*

*and he went in.*

*BEFORE*

*when she opened her arms*

*opened her vagina,*

*he possessed her body.*

*but never her heart.*

*NOW*

*the deception was complete*

*She couldn't tell the difference*

*If you can't tell the difference,*

100

*then it really doesn't matter.*

*HE*

*needed her soul.*

*His soul went out*

*when his drugs went in.*

*Vampirism.*

*And the drain begins.*


POEM    By Bette Richards

WHO LAUGHED BUT ME

*I wonder*

*Who laughed at me*

*Or did anyone even really see*

*Or was it me who laughed at me*

*Laughed to cover up my anxiety*

*Laughed to keep from lyin' and cryin'*

*Rather see a comedy*

*Than a downright tragedy*

`                    ~~~~~~~~~~~~~~~~~~

My brother, Danny, called to inform me, "Dad is dying…he is in Intensive Care at Santa Monica Hospital".

I went there immediately. Danny and Mom were at Dad's bedside. Dad was "out of it". When I arrived, Danny said, "Mom and I are going to get a bite to eat; we've been here all morning."

I was left alone with my father. I touched his beautiful, thick, white hair. He opened his eyes and saw me.

His eyes filled up with tears.

He said, "I'm…..sorry…."

And his eyes closed.

I started singing softly to him…and as I was singing, he passed away.

My father was a strong male role model for me as a child, and we had a very good relationship then. After the scandal and barrage of accusations that occurred with Cookie Gilchrist, and my dad's reaction, I lost that relationship forever.

A void was created that was never filled by another man.

# Chapter Eleven

SHE BETTER NOT BE WHITE!

A Visit to Cookie's House: Philadelphia


It was late 1993, and I finally decided to gather all of my thousands of notes together and tell my story of the false arrest of Cookie Gilchrist and myself. I contacted Cookie because I wanted to offer him the respect needed before I told our story.

So I called him.

He answered, excited to hear from me. He said, "Hold the phone, Bette Ann, hold the phone". He had dropped the phone to go get a letter he had received from the president of ESPN.

I said, "What is ESPN?"

He explained that the television sports channel wanted to do a documentary on him called *"Where Are They Now?"* *He had played for the Buffalo Bills, Denver Broncos, and Miami Dolphins.* They would bring a film crew anywhere he would like.

"The bottom line is that they want to steal my story, Bette Ann. We'll put our stories together and do it without them because those motherfuckers will just rip us off. We will tell it together, Bette Ann...you back me...I back you. I have lawyers, public relations people..." He went on.

I knew little of that business myself, so I agreed.

I was in Los Angeles and Cookie was living in Philadelphia. We began discussing our story by telephone. After about three months of brain-storming our plan, Cookie felt we needed to be in the same city to continue. He invited me to his home where we would combine our stories.

I flew to Philadelphia. When I arrived, he was cordial and polite while showing me to the guest room, a bedroom across the hall from his bedroom on the second floor.

Cookie had aged. He was thin and bald, and did not look anything like the man I once knew.

He asked for a contribution for groceries and he said he would do the cooking, which was just fine with me. I left $400 in his "food kitty", a can on the kitchen table.

He took me up to the third floor where we would collaborate. It was filled with his trophies, newspaper and magazine clippings, and a large collection of memorabilia from his football career.

We began our work. I showed him 300 pages of my writings and we plowed through his materials: hundreds of clippings and photographs.

While working with him, I noticed he did not allow any questions but would instead give me orders. I was used to taking orders in the past from bosses at many different office jobs and I was still unassertive and withdrawn.

Cookie was making and receiving calls day and night. And from my room, I could hear his voice during his phone conversations

I heard him phone Howard Cosell, calling him "collect" several times and Cosell would take his call. He made calls to an executive at ESPN, John Walsh; to some vice presidents at Buffalo Bills; to a curator of the Football Hall of Fame; and many calls to

Jack Kemp, a retired quarterback with the Buffalo Bills and also U. S. Representative; and other famous celebrities.

I would hear him talking, laughing, arguing with these different people.

When we weren't working, I stayed to myself in my room.

And I felt more isolated than ever.

After working together for ten days, I informed Cookie that I needed to take care of some business at the Social Security Office.   He gave me directions on how to take a bus downtown. I went out into the cold December snow and was gone all day.

When I returned, I went upstairs to my room and noticed that Cookie had moved a heavy dresser that I had admired earlier into my bedroom.

He was behaving in a strange manner. His movements were manic.

Then he said to me, "Who did you talk to out there, Bette Ann?"

I answered, "No one, Cookie. Who would I talk to?  I don't know anyone in this town".

He said, "You know they're *watching* us,  Bette Ann.  I've lived here for four years and you are the first person that's ever gotten past the front door".

I repeated, slowly, "No. One. Is. Watching. Us, Cookie."

At that moment some static came through the music that was playing on the radio.

Cookie said "See that! See that, Bette Ann! They're *listening* to us!"

I started to deny….. "No…one…is…listening…to…us, Cookie."

He shrieked like a banshee and screamed, "Shut up, bitch! Did I *tell* you you can talk?!"

Then I knew. Oh My God. He had become paranoid and was flipping out. He had *never* talked to me like this. He always had a protective regard and respect for me.

I shut up.

He walked toward his room, calling me to come. Frightened, I obeyed and followed.

He sat down on the edge of his bed and started on a verbal tirade while I stood there, not taking my eyes off him.

Cookie ranted, "I have a right to do anything and be justified, Bette Ann. No questions. No debating. No arguments."

He went on talking about his spiritual guides.

He said, "They are all against me, Bette Ann! Bette Ann, we are the alpha and omega, Bette Ann, first and last…beginning and ending…start and finish."

Then, he asked me to apply some salve medication to his back which was covered with scabs from ichthyosis vulgaris ("alligator skin" disease).

I was horrified, but at the same time I was overcome with a strong compassion for Cookie. I knew where that pain came from.

As I took the tube of salve and spread it on his shoulders and his back, he repeated, "Bette Ann, we are the alpha and omega, Bette Ann. First and last… beginning and ending …start and finish".

At this point, he rose from the bed, went over to a chest of drawers, opened the bottom one, and took out a machete. He leaned it against the wall.

Then he sat back down on the bed, leaning up against the headboard and told me to go into his study which was adjacent to his bedroom, and ordered me to type a letter to the mayor of Philadelphia.

In a state of paralyzed fear, I obeyed and went into his study, sat down at the typewriter, and pretended to type.

He started to dictate.

*I, Chester Carlton Gilchrist, demand reparation payment for injuries, redress for wrongs done to me when I was stolen by the NFL from the 11th grade for $5000 to play professional football, and when I was sold to R.C. Wilson, Jr., slaveholder of the Buffalo Bills for $30,000.*

I can remember only that much, but he went on and on.

He stopped the dictation and said, "Bette Ann, if they cannot control you, they try to buy you. If they cannot buy you, they will discredit you, and if they cannot discredit you, they will kill you."

After several minutes, I stopped pretending to type but he went on and on.

I thought, "Dear God, the years have driven him to this. I remembered the robust, fun-loving man he once was and now was gone.

He could lock me up on that third floor...no one knows I am here....

I got up and walked back toward his room and entered. I walked over to Cookie, stared straight into his eyes, and said softly, "Cookie, .... I need to.... get... some... air. I don't feel well."

Aware of the risk I was taking, I continue to stare dead into his eyes as he stared back into mine. Our eyes locked.

107

Without a word, he nodded his head slowly and replied…"OK."

I went to my room, put on my coat, took the house keys he had given to me but I could not take my handbag because that might trigger his fear and set him off.

Slowly, I walked down the stairs and fled from the house.

I waved down a passing car and asked the driver for a ride to the Greyhound bus station, explaining that I was visiting from Los Angeles, that my friend was ill and having some kind of psychotic paranoid episode, and I was afraid to go back in that house. The driver very kindly took me to the bus station.

I called a friend in New York City, explained what happened. I didn't want to go back into Cookie's house. She agreed that I should not go back. She suggested I come to her place on the Lower East Side.

I had always carried a folded $20 bill in my pants pocket. With it, I bought a one-way ticket, and was on my way.

When I got to New York, I called a musician friend, Don Moore, and told him what had happened. Don was also a psychiatric social worker, and he urged me to call Cookie, confront him, and demand that he send my belongings and my writings.

I called Cookie, spoke gently and gave him an address of a store front on First Avenue where he should send my suitcases. I also gave him the phone number of the friend where I would be staying.

The next day, a call came from Cookie. He had come to New York City and was in Grand Central Station.

He said, " Come back, Bette Ann, come back. We have to finish the book."

I pleaded, "No, Cookie." With pain in my heart, I told him, "I cannot come back."

You terrified me.  I said goodbye.

He did not call again.

I stayed in New York for a month at that friend's apartment.  She was rarely there.  I had not been in touch with her for some years and when she learned that I was out of money, she was not happy.  I was offered a floor mat to sleep on, and  baked potatoes and brussell sprouts which was left each night for me. I had to wait for some money due to come into my bank account to enable me to buy the plane ticket back to Los Angeles.

My writings, my best clothes, and my jewelry, were all left in Philadelphia.

Cookie finally did ship my suitcases to Los Angeles but they never arrived.  UPS claimed they were lost en route and I collected only $200 for the two lost suitcases.

~~~~~~~~~~~~~~~~

A few months later, I received a phone call from Cookie.

He began the conversation with "We are soulmates, Bette Ann.  We have not prostituted ourselves.  The others sold their souls.  We were together in a past life, Bette Ann.  We have been lovers in a spiritual sense.  A priest from Pittsburgh, Monsignor Charles Owens Rich, maintained that our story has the ingredients to right the erroneous beliefs of society."

Cookie continued to rant.  "You are a ten of Clubs, you are a black woman, Bette Ann.  I'm your protector and your provider."

Cookie repeated this to me over and over again. He continued on, "No one is to blame for what happened to us. That's our karma. They conspired against us to arrest us. It deprived me of an education and we were denied the possibility to get good jobs. They used me as a slave. I told Jim Brown that if I had stayed in Cleveland, nobody would have heard of Jim Brown. They complain, 'Every time we come at this nigger, he got something to say.' That's why they won't let me get an education. But I don't need them, they need me. They've got to come through me. God set it up that way. I did not have anything to do with it. I'm just playing my part. God's taking care of me. 'They' knew that. The white man says of me 'if God ain't taking care of him, we know the devil ain't…otherwise he'd be here with us!."

I was writing down everything he was saying as I quietly listened.

Then I spoke and told him that I had never received my things. To my surprise, he said that he was glad he had not put my writings, notes and manuscript in my suitcase because they would have been lost also.

Another call came from him on April 24, 1999.

"Hello, Bette Ann. This is Cookie. I'm calling to ask you to sell your story to me. But first, do you know what day this is? It's our anniversary. Forty-five years since our arrest on April 24, 1954 at 10:30 pm in New Kensington, PA.

Cookie wanted me to give him my story in exchange for stock in his company, C G Investments. The stock had no value at this time.

I said, "I'm not interested."

We got into an argument. He asked me how much would I want for my story and I said glibly, "Two million and a half". He responded he would give me that much in stock.

When again, I declined, he called me "Bitch!"

He said he would tell his story and refer to me as a "white girl student from Brackenridge."

We had previously agreed to tell our stories together.

Cookie went on…"Bette Ann, I was paraded around the country as a big dumb jock. Because it was done to me, I have a right to do anything."

"Botte Ann, your role is to say 'Amen!'"

~~~~~~~~~~~~~~~~

Another phone call from Cookie on July 27, 2000.

As he began to talk, I began to write.

"I am laying the beachhead for us, Bette Ann. To reassure you, I only think one way. That is positive. Our God instilled in us the energy that says two heads are better than one. But we have to be on the same page. When I grew up, you are seen but not heard. If I tell you something and you don't do it, you are telling me you are smarter than me. Here's how I see it. I have my documents of everything. You can corroborate what I said. Everyone from back then is dead now. Policemen, witnesses, and so forth. You and I know what happened…God sent us here to be each others's testimony. The hook is that we never had sex. I am intimidating to white males, Bette Ann, so you

111

have to lead. It's a dog and pony show. I don't lie to them, Bette Ann, and that's too much power for any black man to have in America. I know how the white man thinks. I say let's you and me get the job done. As a professional, take my feelings and considerations. Let's get un-personal and put aside our egos and make some money. My football experience…I did that because I got paid. If I am not a multi-millionaire, fuck the Hall of Fame, don't put me in no Hall of Fame, no trophies.

"What's mine is mine and what's yours is mine also, Bette Ann. I don't permit anybody to ask me questions. If I say 'jump', you say 'how high? Accept me as I am because I ain't changing".

I listened to every one of his words. Both our hearts had been broken, and his was pouring out. The hurt was deep and it manifested in this kind of pain.

The call was ending with me saying, "I've got to go now, Cookie…" .

As I was hanging up, Cookie was saying he still remembers the dress I was wearing *that night.*

~~~~~~~~~~~~~~~~~

Cookie and I were never romantically involved. We were school classmates who were thrown together to experience a terrible tragedy of hate and the insanity of racism that affected our entire lives. We had a special bond because of the innocence of that which we were accused. Two years my senior, Cookie had a protective attitude toward me and became like a big brother checking up on me throughout the years.

Cookie and I experienced irreparable loss that night of the arrest.  At times, rage and fear ran his life and mine.

In our very different ways, we were unable to trust.

Should I tell the story myself?

Cookie didn't think so - - not without him.

# Chapter TWELVE

## Afterwards

### Call You My Father

Having had no contact with Cookie for several years, I was surprised to received

phone messages from him followed by an e-mail in May of 2000. He wanted to know if I

would be going to our Har-Brack High School 45th Reunion.

Here are copies of the emails::

From: JahShuRaYaMunga@aol.com  (Cookie Gilchrist)

Date: Mon. 15 May2000 22:10:02 EDTSubject: happy belated

birthday.mar.26, 2000

To:bmarrowbone@yahoo.com
I just received your two messages. Thanks for phoning me back.
How are you? When I phoned, I wanted to know if you are coming
to Har-Brack's 45th Reunion? I received an invitation some
months ago. But have not made up my mind about going. It is on
my birthday, May 24,2000
Yvonne Cannon Stewart phone to inquire about my going and in our
conversation, your name came up. I told her the "Truth Is
Interpreted As A Lie and A Lie Is Interpreted As The Truth!
case in point: Betty Ann and I never had any of sex." She
refused to believe what I told her. These lie's have persisted
now for forty-five years. That is a long time to be lied on!"
Don't you agree?
E-mail me back upon receiving this note MS Betty Ann Richards

To Cookie Gilchrist: 11:20 PM  5/15/00 - 0700, No Subject
To: Cookie Gilchrist
From Bette <bmarrowbone@yahoo.com>

So it was really you…

How have you been?  I was surprised to hear from you, and it was a nice surprise at that.  There is no other voice like yours. Thank you for your the birthday greetings. If you will send me a picture of you, I'll send you one of me taken on my birthday. Remember the photo of you that I showed you that I liked so much?  That's the one I'd like as I knew you when we were young. As far as going to the high school reunion,I am not financially able, and although my cousin, Helen invited me to stay with her in her Sheldon Park apt, I would not feel safe there in Pennsylvania.  It is still Klan territory.  The only way I would consider returning was to be incognito and no one would know who I am.

Your old girlfriend and the rest of them back there will never understand us and I don't care.  You and I best understand each other.  Who cares what others think of us.  They will have no credence in my life.  Who are they to you?  Why do they carry any weight in your heart?

So, Mr. Chester Carlton Gilchrist, bye for now and God bless. BettyAnn

I chose not to attend.  Afraid I would still be considered a pariah, an outcast.

Some of the townspeople ignorantly assumed that Cookie was the father of my children.

115

That long ago event raised its ugly head among Cookie and his teammates who were at the Reunion. In no uncertain terms, Cookie told them that there was never a sexual relationship between him and me.

He also added, "Bette Ann is as pure as the driven snow."

This touched my heart and I bless Cookie's sweet heart for speaking up and setting them straight.

When I heard of this from Bernice Miller whose sister was married to one of those football players, I asked one of their teammates if that was true. And if so, would he put that in writing for me.

He consented to do so.

A copy of his letter to me follows at the end of this chapter.

Then in August 2000, I heard from Cookie again. He phoned and asked if I would work for him as an administrative assistant, and tell our story together backing each other up. He would have complete control over the project. I sent him the following response:

> I *deeply and completely understand your rejection of allowing anyone to use you for their benefit and gain. And I agree with the stand you take in maintaining control of everything that concerns you.*
>
> *There are constant attempts by others to place me in the role of* "assistant". *Please reconsider that label "administrative assistant".*
>
> *I will listen to everything you say, but I must maintain separate and individual control of the life that God gave me.*

This was the last communication between Cookie and me.

At 6:20 pm, on January 10, 2011, a classmate from our home town phoned to inform me that Cookie had died.

That year Cookie's sons, Scott and Jeffrey Gilchrist, published the story of Cookie's football career called *The Cookie That Would Not Crumble*. In the book, there is an inaccurate reference to my relationship with Cookie claiming that we were "dating".

Months later, I received a call from Scott, who lives in Toronto. He and his family were making a documentary about Cookie. Scott offered to fly me to Buffalo, New York to participate in the filming. Since I did not want to travel at that time, Scott brought a film crew from Canada to my home.

The documentary is called *Misunderstood: The Cookie Gilchrist Story*.

It was sold on Amazon and is available now from Cookie's younger son, Scott at this address:

scottgilchrist1@msn.com

~~~~~~~~~~~~~~~~~~

I realize now that upon my meeting Booker Little, his calm, conservative presence was a soothing balm to my every pain and because of that, it transformed my life at that time.

One of my grave sins was when I ran away from Booker because he felt that our baby was "a big tie". At that time, I understood it then as a big negative. Today I believe that had he lived, he would have taken care of me and our child . He was too good a man to have left us.   It was I who ran away from him.

Booker lived and breathed his music as he practiced and wrote every day. He was a virtuoso on his instrument, the beloved trumpet.

Booker's name is listed in all the encyclopedias, and his recordings are available all over the world.

~~~~~~~~~~~~~~~~~~~

My sister, Esther suffered from scleroderma and passed away in 2015.

Even though she had been very ill, she had kept hopes that we could sing together again. She would lament, "Just one more time, Betts, just one more time."

We had some great times together in spite of our occasional feuds, and when we sang together, we sang as "one".

But *my singing other half* is gone.

.

~~~~~~~~~~~~~~~~~~~

My children, Ann, William and Dala, grown up now, live all across the country in various states.  Among them I am blessed to have nine grandchildren.  Eight boys and one girl.

Interracial relationship still is *an unwritten sin* in many minds today.  It is the tenor of the times: on the surface, people appear to be getting along; but scratch the surface and you will touch a nerve.  Does the white man want to see his daughter with a black man?  Does the black woman want to see her son with a white woman?

Living among blacks, I heard the creativity of their music, witnessed their athletic prowess, and their indomitable souls.  I came to deeply appreciate that strength and beauty and their struggles.

~~~~~~~~~~~~~~~~~

Another grave sin was to not have honored my father when he said 'no', and he didn't want me being a majorette. He did not want his daughter prancing around with bare legs, displaying her body half-dressed, wearing a skirt so short.  I disobeyed him and defied him through my mother, begging her to intercede for my wishes.

Looking back, I see my father arriving in Los Angeles after a turbulent flight.  He had become very sick and was wheeled from the plane.  He saw me and started crying.

"I'm sorry, Bette Ann, I'm sorry". He did not clarify to me what he was sorry about, and I believe he did not have the words.

My friend, Don, the musician and psychiatric social worker, said to me recently, "As long as I have known you, you wanted to be taken care of."

I secretly thought, "Is it frightening for me to let myself be taken care of?"

One day, I asked, "Don, out of all the many musicians I've known, some did desire me, but why didn't any one of them want to marry me - stay with me - to call me their own?

Don answered, "Because you were one of the fellas! ".

That shocked me.

Stunned at his response, I was speechless, dumbfounded.

119

Lying awake in bed that night, tears came rolling down into my ears as I sobbed and boo-hooed, "I don't want to be a fella! I don't want to be a fella!

"*Ain't I A Woman?*"

As I am writing this story and looking back, I am seeing many areas where I was on automatic pilot much of the time with no conscious thought. Being somewhat conscious now, I have come to some awareness.

Most importantly, I met a clergyman who *listened.*

He listened, and it drew me back to God.

I became reconciled with the grief that I carried over losing my father.

Returning to my roots, I contacted local musicians and recorded three albums, the genre of gospel/country/blues, at a home recording studio. I had sidewalk sales of old furniture to bankroll the project called:

**Gospel at Sheepskin Flat Road, Volume One, Two, & Three**

~~~~~~~~~~~~~~~~

A memory from many years ago...

A little girl stands over the heat register in her bedroom, dressed in her nightgown, holding a flashlight, pretending it was a microphone. She sings away, imagining herself a grown-up singer.

Today that same singer sings along with a recording as she cries, "Father! Father! Call You my Father! I reach out my hand to Thee..."

~~~~~~~~~~~~~~~~~

The ontological loneliness still overtakes me at times.

Always at twilight...

when the sun is going down

when the window blinds are closing for the night...

120

"For there is a shame that brings sin, and there is a shame that brings glory and grace."

from RSV: Ecclesiasticus iv, 21

GOSPEL
at Sheepskin Flat Road

BETTE
RICHARDS

NORTH RECORDING STUDIO

ENTRANCE

GOSPEL at
SHEEPSKIN
FLAT
ROAD

BetteAnn
Richards

**Eugene Capriotti, Cookie Gilchrist, and Frank Corso at the Har-Brack 45th Class - Reunion; August 26, 2000**

Friday, September 14, 2012

Dear Betty Ann,

You tell me that in the book "The Cookie that wouldn't Crumble" reference is made to a romantic relationship between Cookie Gilchrist and you. Not only have you told me that is not true, so did Cookie himself; several times as a matter of fact. He seemed obsessed with the need to tell everyone he could that he never had a sexual relationship with you. When talking to several former football teammates at the 2000 reunion of the Har-Brack High School class of 1955, he was adament on the subject. He never had sex with Betty Ann Richards. Period. His words!

I hope that all is going well with you.

Best Regards, Eugene R. Capriotti

## At 3 years old

## Mother and Me

There was a little girl
who had a little curl
right in the middle of her forehead
and when she was good
she
was
criticized
anyway.